Intentional Dis

and Disciple-Making

An Anglican Guide for Christian Life and Formation

Published by The Anglican Consultative Council
London 2016

ISBN 978-0-9566596-4-4

Published by The Anglican Consultative Council

Edited by The Revd Canon John Kafwanka and the Revd Canon Mark Oxbrow

Set in Adobe Caslon Pro 12/ 14.4

Anglican Witness

Intentional Discipleship and Disciple-Making

Follow me

and I will make you fish

for people

(Mk 1.17)

Foreword by the Archbishop of the Province of South East Asia

'Follow me'. These two simple words of invitation and command stand at the head of every relationship with Jesus, the Son of God, whether spoken on a Galilean lake shore, on the streets of Lusaka, or in a hospital in Chicago. Like every child responding to the outstretched hand of a parent, Simon and Andrew, Mary and Salome, and millions of Christians through two millennia have accepted that simple invitation in faith and often with minimal understanding of the life-transforming decision they have taken. To follow Jesus of Nazareth into his cosmic reign is simply the most challenging, the most beautiful, the most costly, the most rewarding journey we could ever choose to begin.

Visit any province in the Anglican Communion today and in each place you will be struck by the courage, faithfulness, and love with which our Anglican people are following Jesus. As Peter discovered on his journey up to Jerusalem, the road ahead is not always clear, and as James and John discovered there are temptations of power and influence. Some of us have even found ourselves as compromised as Judas, but the overwhelming impression I have of our Communion is that of a beautifully diverse family of women, men, and children who are deeply in love with Jesus and seeking daily to follow in his ways.

Whether we speak in terms of discipleship or apostleship, a dynamic discussed in this book, our following Jesus requires much more than the latest course or introduction to Christian living. Courses have their place, and many excellent resources are mentioned in the pages that follow, but our apostleship, our discipleship, demands much more – in fact it demands everything. As you will know, the three priorities chosen by Archbishop Justin Welby for his tenure as Archbishop of Canterbury are the renewal of prayer and religious life, evangelism, and reconciliation. I believe that these three priorities help us to unpack the invitation to discipleship. Firstly it is an invitation to an increasingly intimate relationship with the Triune God whom we know in Jesus. This relationship, which is both individual and communal, is nurtured through prayer and the deepening of spiritual life. As together we go on following the ways of Jesus we discover, with Paul, that our life becomes less and less our own and increasingly 'hidden with Christ in God' (Col 3.3). In stark contrast to the individualism that plagues much of our contemporary society, we find ourselves becoming part of something (someone) much greater, much more beautiful and fulfilling. But this experience of true humanity 'in God' is not something to hold to ourselves. It is for all humanity, indeed for all creation (Rom 8.19).

The invitation to follow is, in the Gospels, immediately followed by a promise which is often misunderstood as a command or authorization – 'I will make you fishers of [people].' Evangelism is not a task given to the Church, but a promise. Jesus promises that as we follow him we will become fishers of men, women, and children. Our lives, reflecting the image of God, will attract and change others. To hold the good news of the Gospel of Jesus Christ to ourselves is a supreme act of selfishness. As we follow and are shaped by the life of Jesus, that selfish possessiveness of our relationship with him will be dissipated and we will naturally begin to include others in that love-relationship. Exclusivity has no place in the family of God; all God-centred relationships are inclusive, and our evangelism has nothing to do with numbers and power but everything to do with love, generosity, inclusion, and the all-encompassing life and love of God.

As our daily following of Jesus, our apostolic vocation, draws us deeper into the Body of Christ, the life of the Triune God, reconciliation becomes a pressing priority. Humanity shares the brokenness and pain of our world, and this needs to be brought to God, to be offered at the Cross – to find reconciliation, wholeness, and life in the shattered life of God. As Paul reminds us, the heart of our discipleship is not only to 'be reconciled' with God but also to exercise a 'ministry of reconciliation' (2 Cor 5.11–21). That ministry is to be exercised within the Church, in the wider community, and in our relationship with the whole created order. In many ways this life of reconciliation is the most public aspect of our Christian discipleship and at the same time deeply enmeshed with our witness, or evangelism.

As a Communion we are profoundly in need of reconciliation and we find ourselves in a world equally riven by fear, division, and brokenness. It is for this reason that, as never before, we need to accept Jesus' invitation to an apostleship, a discipleship, of the whole of our lives. A narrow, pietistic attachment to Jesus, whether individualistic or ecclesial, was never what God intended and will not serve us well today. Following Jesus will and must change every aspect of our being. At the core will be our reconciliation with God, but this can never be complete until we are at peace with ourselves, in vital communion with the whole Body of Christ, in a renewed relationship with the whole human family, and discovering a new harmony with creation as a whole. Wrestling with environmental issues, with peace-building and peace-keeping, with the complexities of human relationships, with truth, justice, and loving, and with the care of our family and ourselves – these are all key concerns for those who accept the invitation of Jesus to 'follow'.

I welcome this careful study of the way discipleship has been understood and practised in the Christian Church, and not least in the Anglican Communion, and I commend it to you as an inspiration and guide for a deepening of our apostolic vocation as we, members of the One, Holy, Catholic, Apostolic Church, joyfully accept the invitation to follow Jesus and the promise that we will become 'fishers' of the many more to whom Jesus extends his same gracious invitation today.

The Most Revd Ng Moon Hing

Bishop of the Diocese of West Malaysia and Primate of the Church of the Province of South East Asia

Easter 2016

Preface

> The best decision anyone can ever make, at any point in life, in any circumstances, whoever they are, wherever they are, is to become a disciple of Jesus Christ
>
> *Archbishop Justin Welby*

Following concerns expressed by the Lambeth Conference in 2008, the ACC-14 in 2009 requested the Secretary General to set up an Evangelism and Church Growth Initiative (now known as Anglican Witness: Evangelism and Church Growth Initiative of the Anglican Communion) to spearhead research, thinking, and action within the Communion.

This book developed out of the work of the Anglican Witness Core Group, and particularly the encouragement and endorsement by the Standing Committee in May 2014 for the Mission Department to 'focus on discipleship', and the request to prepare a formal proposal for the same.

In September 2015, a paper entitled 'Intentional Discipleship and Disciple-Making', a background paper for ACC-16, articulating a theological rationale for discipleship, was presented to the Standing Committee. The paper, which is the basis for this book, was very warmly received, and the Archbishop of Canterbury described it as the 'best document I have read on the subject'.

Inspired by the discussion which resulted from the paper, the Standing Committee recommended Intentional Discipleship in a World of Differences as a theme for the ACC-16 in April 2016.

Focus on discipleship has become both common and relevant among many Christian traditions in the light of the unprecedented challenges we now face, raising the question of the role of Christian faith in a world where potential lives side by side with the immense challenges of our time. These include the constant threat of conflict among nations and peoples, including religious and ethnically motivated violence, increase in economic deprivation among communities, erosion of integrity and widespread corruption in many nations, and the challenge of climate change and environmental degradation among many others.

Needless to say, Anglicans/Episcopalians are witnessing to Christ's reconciling love all over the world, and in all sorts of ways, as a sign of their discipleship. But many Anglican/Episcopalian leaders, lay and ordained, are also quick to point out that much more could be done if there was an intentional focus on nurturing and equipping both new and existing members, to deepen their lifelong discipleship and Christian witness.

As would be expected, there is a rich diversity in the understanding and practice of discipleship and disciple-making within the contemporary life of the Communion. In some contexts there is a strong intentionality about this ministry, whereas in others the Church needs to be called back to its roots as a community of disciples who make disciples.

Bishop Steven Croft of Sheffield Diocese in England acknowledged that the 'Vatican Synod of Bishops (called by Pope Francis 2014) revealed that the church throughout the world has same struggles to communicate faith, and it's not just Europe and America (or the West) but even where the Church is growing. There is need to listen and learn from each other within the Body of Christ.'

This book brings together research, experience, and aspirations from theologians and mission leaders around the Anglican Communion. It seeks to stimulate further reflection and presents a foundation for thinking about discipleship and disciple-making as the Church's primary mandate given by Jesus Christ under the empowerment of the Holy Spirit.

The book is not complete in itself or in any way, but is offered as a resource to foster what must come naturally as central to the being and character of the Church, not just when it is convenient but in every sphere of the life of all the baptized.

Special thanks go to many theologians and church leaders from around and beyond the Anglican Communion who contributed to this publication, for their passion to see that all Anglicans/Episcopalians strive to be faithful followers of Jesus Christ in every sphere of life and are equipped for social and community transformation empowered by the Gospel of Christ and to the glory of God.

Contents

Foreword by the Archbishop of the Province of South East Asia vii
Preface xi

Part A Theological Background 1

Introduction 3
Chapter 1 A Biblical Theology of Disciple-Making 9
Chapter 2 Discipleship in the Early Church 25
Chapter 3 Recent Roman Catholic Theology of Disciple-Making 31
Chapter 4 Discipleship in the Orthodox Tradition 35
Chapter 5 History of Anglican Formation and Discipleship 37
Chapter 6 The Five Marks of Mission 47
Chapter 7 Healing and Discipleship 51
Chapter 8 Discipleship and Instruments of Anglican Communion 59

Part B Contemporary Anglican Praxis of Discipleship 77

Introduction 79
Chapter 9 Africa 81
Chapter 10 Asia 87
Chapter 11 Europe 93
Chapter 12 The Americas 97
Chapter 13 An Anglican Discipleship among Children and Youth 107
Chapter 14 The Bible, Worship, Sacraments, and the Eucharistic Community 109
Chapter 15 Resourcing Discipleship? 111
Chapter 16 Mission and Development Agencies 117
Chapter 17 Conclusion: The Case for Intentional Discipleship in the Communion 125

Part A
Theological Background

Introduction

This book has been prepared by a group of Anglican leaders and theologians as a resource for the Anglican Consultative Council discussion on discipleship (ACC-16), and for the Communion more widely. The views expressed are sometimes those of individuals and sometimes corporate but together they represent the broad sweep of thinking within the Communion. In this way the book seeks to draw particularly on historic Anglican theology but also acknowledges the great wealth of thinking on this topic within the wider Christian community.

The wider context for our thinking about *intentional* Christian discipleship and disciple-making is the eternal mission of the Triune God, the Missio Dei, the redemptive love of Creator for creature, which is both the river pouring life into our daily walk with God and the sea into which we offer our missional intent by the power of the Spirit.[1]

It is very clear from the study of Scriptures, the life of the early Church, and the witness of different Christian traditions over two thousand years that *intentional* discipleship and the regular practice of making disciples are central to our understanding of salvation, mission, and ecclesiology.

Part A of this book provides a comprehensive survey of this theology and historical practice, provided by a number of Anglican theologians and leaders and followers of Jesus.

Within the contemporary life of the Communion we find a rich diversity in the understanding and practice of discipleship and disciple-making. In some contexts there is a strong *intentionality* about this ministry, whereas in others the Church needs to be called back to its roots as a community of disciples who make disciples.

Part B of this book provides a stimulating overview of this diversity of ministry. The book provides case studies from the different geographical

1 The primary intended meaning of 'Missio Dei' in this text is the Mission of the Triune God, 'Missio Triuni Dei'.

regions, followed by a consideration of the role of children and young people, and the significance of the Bible, worship, Sacraments, and Eucharistic Community for discipleship. This is followed by brief descriptions of some resources which have been found helping in parts of the Communion as they have become more *intentional* in their approach to discipleship and disciple-making.

Terminologies and what they mean

A lot has been written regarding the precise meaning of words and whether a word such as 'mission' should be understood as the whole of a Christian's life of response to God, or a narrow obedience to the Spirit's sending out to proclaim in word and deed the saving acts of God, or the even narrower activities of the Church which facilitate her growth. In the end the use of language is negotiated as part of the process of constructing meaning within a particular human community. To determine the meaning of words becomes even more complex when people use multiple languages. While rejoicing in the diversity of the Anglican Communion, the authors have had to negotiate with each other through translation. In order for them to make sense together in this book, the first point of negotiation was to agree on meanings for the terms 'discipleship' and 'disciple-making', and for the 'intentionality' of both.

The first invitation which Jesus offered to those who showed an interest in his life and teaching was to follow (to be a disciple), and that was quite literally what they did on the roads and through the villages of ancient Palestine. But it was not just a physical following. As we read the Gospel narrative we quickly observe that the 'following' also involves a μετάνοια (a radical turning around) of lifestyle, world-view, and spiritual orientation, a total transformation of the self, so that Paul is led to claim, 'So if anyone is in Christ, there is a new creation: everything old has passed away; see, everything has become new!' (2 Cor 5.17). For the sake of this book we wish to negotiate a meaning for 'discipleship' which encompasses this total God-ward transformation which takes place when individuals and communities intentionally, sacrificially, and consistently live every aspect of their daily life in commitment to following Jesus Christ.

Therefore, to be a disciple is to follow, and the nature of that discipleship is defined by the One we follow. To be a disciple-maker is to have been transformed as we follow him who calls us so that we share in the calling and lifelong transformation of others. 'Follow me, and I will make you fish for people' (Mt 4.19). By 'intentional' we mean a deliberate prioritizing of these actions individually and as a Church – the Christian community. Although Jesus' injunction to his followers to 'go and make disciples' should instil and result in deliberate or intentional action, the common use of the term 'discipleship' often does not communicate the intended intentional 'emphasis', and so the natural and original meaning is often completely lost. Therefore, the use of the word 'intentional' in this text is meant to reclaim the lost emphasis both in usage and also in the practice of both discipleship and disciple-making.

The Orthodox theology of *theosis* (see Chapter 4 below) and Western Christian theology of *sanctification* speak powerfully of this total God-ward transformation which is the final objective of discipleship. Drawing on 2 Peter 1.4 ('you ... may become participants of [or in] the divine nature'), 2 Corinthians 3.18 ('And all of us, with unveiled faces, seeing the glory of the Lord as though reflected in a mirror, are being transformed into the same image from one degree of glory to another'), and similar texts, we understand *theosis* not as 'deification' (man becoming God) but rather as the outpouring of God's life into our lives so that day by day we more clearly reflect God's glory, being ourselves made more fully alive, truly human. As such, discipleship is a lifelong, whole-life reorientation which will have challenging implications for our self-identity, our belonging within community, our belief systems, and our daily behaviour.

This is the kind of discipleship we have in mind for Anglicans and the Anglican Communion. It is about steering a course for a Communion in which every member has a daily intention to follow Christ in every aspect of their lives, come what may.

So what about 'disciple-making'? The definition in this book is not about courses of training, or church programmes, or mentoring schemes for discipleship-making (although all of these may have a valuable part to play).

This is about a very natural process of reproduction. Not addition (building up the Church or ensuring that a nation has more Christians than Muslims, for example) or multiplication (programmes of church growth) but the natural process through which infectious Christ-like living attracts and brings forth new life, new discipleship in others. A church of healthy disciples should not need disciple-making programmes, because disciple-making and discipleship are a natural outcome as disciples live as intentional followers of Jesus Christ. Plentiful, committed, loving, and responsible disciple-making activity is a sure sign of healthy disciples and discipleship in action within a church and the Communion as a whole, and the outcome of that will be new disciples. Therefore, where Christians live out their faith ('intentional' discipleship), new disciples are formed (disciple-making), to the extent that discipleship and disciple-making are a product of each other.

Discipleship and the whole life of the whole people of God

Discipleship can never be about a single aspect of our lives, or behaviour, or religious expression. It is (in the definition used in this book) about the whole of the life of a Christian[2] and the Christian community, and this means the whole people of God, young and old, lay and clergy, and in everything they do and say on a daily basis. God's will is that as adults become disciples, so do children, youth, and young adults become disciples of Jesus and disciple-makers, as also those who are differently abled both physically and mentally.

Meanwhile, intentionally following Jesus Christ will place demands upon individuals, our family relationships, the way we handle money, our attitude towards employment and leisure activities, our exploitation of the environment, our political choices, and much more.

2 Every follower of Jesus will need to live in their everyday life the implications of following him because, as N. T. Wright asserts, 'the question of Jesus – who he really was, what he really did, what it means, and why it matters – remains hugely important in every area, not only in personal life, but also in political life, not only in "religion" or "spirituality", but also in … culture, justice, beauty, ecology, friendship, scholarship, and sex'. N. T. Wright, Simply Jesus (London: SPCK, 2011), p. 7.

Intentional discipleship is radically transformative of the whole of life. It is the totality of our living in God, through the power of the Holy Spirit following the ways of Jesus – and that demands internal coherence.

As has been argued above, there is also incoherence in our discipleship if *intentional* disciple-making of others does not follow. This may be a shared process within the local Body of Christ, but where new life is missing the presence of living discipleship may be in doubt.

Disciple-making is not convert-making. In other words, new disciples need to be discipled, not left to fend for themselves. Being discipled and discipling others is a lifelong journey as we follow Jesus Christ, acting on his words, and walking in his ways towards a deeper redeemed relationship with God, being 'changed from one degree of glory to another' as we walk more closely with him and each other.

Intentional or *intentionality* means making a purposeful commitment to a personal relationship with Jesus Christ, who also sends us out in the world to be an instrument of God and God's love for and in his world.[3] Life shaped by a personal relationship with Jesus Christ is a life nourished by prayer and study of Scripture, empowered by the Holy Spirit for the life of service (in every sphere of life). One's whole life, with humility, speaks with boldness in witness to one's faith in Christ and his love for the world.

All language has to be negotiated, and while some Anglicans will be more at home in Swahili than in Spanish, others will prefer to talk of 'living in holiness' or '*theosis*' or 'Christian life and living' rather than of discipleship. Readers of this book should be free to translate 'discipleship' and 'disciple-making' into their own mother tongue or theological tradition, not forgetting our stress on *intentionality* for equipping and in living one's faith in everyday life to the honour and glory of God.

3 Mk 3.14–15; 6.7–13; 16.15. At the heart of Christian discipleship is the understanding that Jesus Christ (the Master) sends out his followers into the world to proclaim the Good News and the coming Kingdom.

Finally, it must be made clear that making more disciples is not the goal of mission, discipleship, or disciple-making. Rather, discipleship and the making of disciples are the natural outcome and expression of mission, and the sole goal of discipleship and mission is to honour and glorify God – experienced as God's reign and also manifest in the lives and actions of the disciples (a sign of God's reign).[4] Making disciples is part of the journey, the Way, towards that eternal goal.

4 'My Father is glorified by this, that you bear much fruit and become my disciples' (Jn 15.8).

Chapter 1 – A Biblical Theology of Disciple-Making

Disciple-making in the Old Testament

The reality of being a disciple is probably best seen in the Old Testament with a call 'to walk in all his ways, to love him, to serve the Lord your God with all your heart and with all your soul' (Deut 10.12–13 et al.). That includes keeping to God's instructions, but also imitating or reflecting God's character. Israel, as a whole people, was called to that kind of discipleship, by living as the people of YHWH in the midst of the nations, being faithful to its covenant with him, worshipping him alone, and living by the standards of the Torah.

Four aspects of such practical discipling are outlined here.

The training and mentoring of a new leader

The Old Testament gives several examples of the transition from one leader to another, in which it seems that the text itself stresses the role of the older one in preparing, training, and mentoring the younger. Moses has Joshua serve under him for a long time, and gives him both encouragement and warning before passing on the baton of leadership (Deut 3.21–22; 31.1–8; 34.9). God himself reinforces the lessons that Moses had taught (Josh 1.1–9). David passes the kingship on to his son Solomon, though in the midst of some very fractured and violent family vendettas. His words (if not his example) amount to encouragement and warning (which Solomon later ignored; 1 Chron 28–29). Elisha accompanies Elijah for some time, doubtless observing and learning, and then goes on to an even longer ministry (1 Kings 19.19–21; 2 Kings 2; 2 Kings 4ff).

The discipline of the family

Deuteronomy stresses the importance of the parents' role in teaching each new generation to walk in the ways of the Lord. This included constant reminders of the story (what God had done in Israel's past) and of the teaching (God's covenant promises and commandments).

Discipling means discipline, and that was part of the function of the wider Israelite household in which individuals found their identity, security, memory, hope, and responsibility (Deut 4.9–14; 6.4–9, 20–25). This is a theme found strongly in the Wisdom Literature too (esp. Prov 1–9).

The teaching impact of the community's worship

Israel had its rich and complex system of worship, which should have functioned as a means of discipling in two ways:

The teaching of the priests: Priests not only brought the sacrifices of the people to the altar. They also were responsible for teaching God's law to the people (Lev 10.8–11; Deut 33.10; Jer 18.18). Their failure in this was a major accusation made by the prophets as they challenged an increasingly untaught and undisciplined people (Hos 4.1–9; Mal 2.1–9).

The didactic impact of the Psalms: Simply by repeated singing of the words of the Psalms (with their history, covenant reminders, condemnation of some behaviours and praise of others, ethical depth and specificity, etc.) faithful Israelites would be shaped in their thinking and practice by the values inculcated in worship.

The shaping function of Scripture

The importance of the reading and dissemination of the written Torah is noted early on. The whole community was to be discipled by hearing and responding to the Word of God, at whatever stage they happened to be engaging with it (Deut 31.9–13). The Psalms celebrate this life-giving, life-enriching, life-shaping force of the Word of God ('law' being an inadequate word for the richness of the Torah; Pss 1, 19, 119). The poet of Psalm 119 celebrates the power of God's Word, in itself, to keep a person on the right path and off the wrong ones.

Nehemiah 8 is a remarkable occasion of community discipling, as the whole law is read through in a week, and trained Levites are on hand to translate, explain, and make clear the meaning of the words read, after which the heads of the families pass it on to their families – perhaps the first example of theological education by extension. The chapter happily points out that the people had abundant joy both when they understood the word of Scripture and when they obeyed it – which is rather close to what discipling involves (Neh 8.12, 17).

Discipleship in the New Testament

The accounts in the Gospels of Jesus the Messiah (the Christ) are inevitably foundational in any quest to discover what is distinctively Christian about discipleship. The Gospels, as it were, take us inside the classrooms within Jesus' 'discipleship school'.

Jesus' public ministry was not a stand-alone performance of ministering solo as the authoritative teacher and healer. Instead, from its outset, we see Jesus intentionally gathering a group of 'learners' who were selected to be with him (Mk 3.16–20). In so doing, he was, at one level, doing nothing different from other rabbis or from John the Baptist, who gathered such disciples around themselves. At another level, because of who we now understand Jesus to be (the Messiah of Israel, the Son of God now risen from the dead), we can discern many further layers to Jesus' intentions.[5] For our present purposes, however, we can note that, in gathering disciples around him throughout his ministry, Jesus was doing two main things which would become perennially important for his followers in generations to come:

(a) He was giving us a model in his own actions of how to be a disciple-maker;

(b) He was allowing his first disciples in their responses towards him to become, for us, a model of how we should respond to

5 For example, in choosing an inner circle of the twelve he was evoking the history the foundational twelve tribes of Israel and thus signalling the reconstitution of Israel around himself. He was also entrusting to them the mandate to remember his teaching and to proclaim it 'to the ends of the earth' (thus in principle commissioning the writings of the New Testament).

Jesus' call and follow him too, revealing the primary hallmark of Christian discipleship (that is, being a learner in Jesus' school, a follower of Jesus).

These two interrelated themes are seen in all the Gospels (though perhaps especially in Mark), which therefore serve as vital and enduring 'manuals of discipleship' for the Christian Church.

Jesus the disciple-maker

In Mark's Gospel we thus see, first, how Jesus does his training of would-be followers. We can observe the Master-Discipler about his trade. In brief we see:

(c) His first calling of the disciples, which is clear and directional, vocational and radical (3.13–19);

(d) His commitment to sharing his life with them;

(e) His intention to give time for de-briefing (6.6b–13, 30–32) and his use of recent events and teachings as an opportunity for further teaching and discussion, helping his followers to process externally what they had experienced (4.35–41; 8.27–30);

(f) His willingness to have an inner circle (Peter, James, and John) who would witness more intimately and directly three momentous events in his life – his rising from the dead, Transfiguration, and Agony (5.37–43; 9.2–8; 14.32–36);

(g) His willingness to chide and admonish, to expose and rebuke his followers, while being totally committed to their growth and restoration (8.17–21; 9.35–37);

(h) His ability to ask questions which would bring to the surface their wrong motivations or muddled ideas (8.17; 9.33–34);

(i) His occasional giving of bizarre instructions which simply had to be obeyed 'because he said so' (but which would make sense later: 11.2–3ff; 14.13–16);

(j) His deliberate policy of letting them see him both in public and in private, both 'on the job' and more intimately 'as a friend'.

(k) All of these will need to be borne in mind whenever we come to ask the contemporary question: how can we be disciple-makers in our own generation?

Following Jesus: in the Gospels

Secondly, we can see in the Gospels how the first disciples responded to Jesus – what they were called to do and thus what we are called to when we respond to Jesus and become his followers today. Here are the hallmarks of authentic Christian discipleship:

Jesus the teacher – we must listen to his words

A rabbi's disciples were first and foremost expected to listen to their rabbi's teaching in public, to discuss it in private afterwards, and, almost certainly, to commit some of its more distinctive aspects to memory. They were in a school; they were students. Jewish disciples were committed to the Old Testament Scriptures, but also to their rabbi's particular 'interpretation' and application of those Scriptures. In the same way we, as followers of the Risen Jesus, are to be students of the words of Jesus, attentive to his living voice, obedient to his principles. We are also to learn his reverent but radical interpretation of the Old Testament Scriptures – namely that they speak of him and he is their ultimate fulfilment.[6]

6 See Lk 24.32; 4.16–22, etc. This commits us to an essentially Christo-centric biblical theology as a matter of our loyal obedience and discipleship of Jesus.

Jesus the person – we must learn from his character

Students learn not just from the actual words of their teachers but also from many other things: for example, watching how they process their thoughts in response to questions and how they handle controversy. They are learning from the teacher's whole demeanour, their character and lifestyle, their response and actions, their tone of voice, and the quality of their life.

For Jesus' first disciples this was their awesome privilege – daily to observe him in action. Here was the truly Human One modelling authentic humanness (as God had intended before the Fall): what an object lesson in how to live! It made a deep impression on John, his 'beloved disciple': 'in him there is no sin' (1 Jn 3.5). And it led to a challenging application: 'whoever says, "I abide in him", ought to walk just as he walked' (1 Jn 2.6).

Christian discipleship today means modelling our lives and characters on Jesus' own; it means living his life. In our own unaided efforts, this is, of course, impossible, but, if Jesus is risen from the dead and he is now through the gift of his Spirit imparting his life-power into us, then we can indeed begin to live his life – drawing upon the power of his life (which has been placed within us). Thus the modern disciple discovers an amazing secret: that the quality and character of that life – which we see Jesus demonstrating in the Gospels – that life is now at work within us, enabling us to live his risen life. The life he once lived becomes the life he now gives. And its patterns and disciplines become ours to live out in our own human existence.

Jesus the leader – we must follow his direction

Jesus said, 'Follow me' (Mk 1.17). From the outset Jesus uses the verb 'to follow' as the primary image for discipleship. It is also his last, acutely personal, command to Peter before the Ascension: 'Follow me!' (repeated for emphasis: Jn 21.19, 22). Evidently, a 'disciple' (learner) must also be a 'follower'.

This then entails the idea that Jesus' disciples are to set out on a journey – on a journey where Jesus is 'out in front' as the leader. We are to go where he leads and to be guided by his navigational directions, even if, like the disciples, we do not always understand where he is leading us. As the Israelites in the desert were to follow the cloud and fire of the Lord's presence (Ex 13.21–22; cf. Num 12.4–5), so Jesus' disciples must follow his presence. For the original twelve there was a literal journey following Jesus up from Galilee into the eye of the storm, Jerusalem – a journey marked with misguided hopes and some trepidation. It certainly filled Thomas with morbid anxiety ('Let us also go, that we may die with him': Jn 11.16) and confusion ('Lord, we do not know where you are going. How can we know the way?': Jn 14.5). However, Jesus assures his disciples that he is to 'go [ahead] to prepare a place' for them and that he himself is the Way (Jn 14.2, 6). In other words: Keep close to me, follow me day by day, and I will ensure that you eventually arrive in that place where you will see me and my glory (see Jn 17.24).

In Hebrews and Revelation this heavenly destination (where Jesus now is) is described as the 'heavenly' or 'new' Jerusalem (Heb 12.22; Rev 3.12; 21.1–2). So it is entirely fitting that the Gospel writers (especially Mark and Luke) see the journey of the original disciples going up to the physical Jerusalem as a model or paradigm for all subsequent disciples: we are all on a journey, following Jesus, all travellers 'on the way' (Mk 8.27; 10.32); we are to leave things behind (Lk 9.57–62); we are to trust him both for our eventual arrival in the city and also for the surprising details along the way and through the desert; above all, we are to 'take up [our] cross daily' and follow Jesus (Lk 9.23).

This following, however, takes the disciples into a mission which will outlast, and in some ways surpass, Jesus' own ministry. Jesus was quite clear that he not only wanted his disciples to go out and minister as he ministered (Mt 10.8) during his lifetime, but that they would 'do the works that I do, and in fact will do greater works than these' (Jn 14.12), and furthermore that he wanted them to teach others to obey all that he had commanded them (Mt 28.19–20). We must address the practical aspects of our obligation to continue the active, Spirit-dependent ministry of Jesus if we are to grasp fully the nature of the discipleship he intended us to pursue. Our task is to continue his mission – which he laid out in Luke 4. Discipleship, following Jesus, is much more than belief and personal growth in Christian character.

This journey therefore requires numerous qualities: self-denial, exposure to risks, setting out in faith, sticking close to Jesus, and actively trusting in his guiding. As some have explained, 'F.A.I.T.H.' requires 'Forging Ahead In Trusting Him'. So being disciples of Jesus is no armchair activity or spectator sport; it is no detached agreement with the teaching principles and moral precepts of a respected teacher (now dead). It is an all-encompassing activity, an all-engaging pursuit which 'demands our life, our soul, our all'. And it is this, so all the Gospel writers unashamedly assert, because the person whom we are called to follow is gloriously alive. Each Gospel climaxes with the confident assertion and proclamation of the Resurrection, leaving its readers with a clear call now to trust and obey this Risen Lord: 'listen to his words', 'learn from his character', and 'follow his leading'. So through the Gospel, the Risen Jesus can say to us what he once said to Peter: 'Follow me' (Jn 21.19).

By way of conclusion we can note how, in an artless way, Mark's Gospel shows how the first followers progressed through each of these three dimensions of discipleship. First they were attracted to the quality of his teaching: 'What is this? A new teaching – with authority!' (Mk 1.22, 27); next to the mysterious quality of his Person: 'Who can forgive sins but God alone?' … that even the wind and the sea obey him? … You are the Messiah' (Mk 2.7; 4.41; 8.29); and finally they were caught up in his purposeful journey towards Jerusalem as they were to 'take up their cross and follow me.' (Mk 8.34; Mk 9–11).

In a sense these three are key ingredients in our following of any human leader: we listen to what they say, we observe who they are, and we evaluate what they do. This can be summarized in various other ways: we focus on their Speech, Person, and Agenda; their Words, Wisdom, and Way.[7]

7 Other summaries include: their Teaching, Tone, and Targets; their Precepts, Person, and Path; their Doctrine, Demeanour, and Direction.

Not surprisingly, therefore, these are key ingredients for Christians seeking to follow the ultimate human, Jesus. In the Gospels we see Jesus masterfully creating a band of faithful disciples through allowing them transparent access to him in each of these three ways. And as the now Risen Lord he offers us today the same access with the same goal – creating faithful disciples.

Following Jesus: in the rest of the New Testament

Yes, Jesus is risen. If Jesus had not been raised bodily from the grave, then all this talk about 'discipleship' – learning to be a follower of Jesus – would have come, quite appropriately, to a sudden and abrupt end. After all, a crucified Messiah was a contradiction in terms. There would have been little purpose or sense in following this Jesus: for, however great his religious teaching, he had evidently failed in the most important task of the Messiah and had been wrong in everything he had claimed for himself.

The Resurrection is thus an essential ingredient in ongoing discipleship. We must abandon any fond ideas that we can somehow read the Gospels and choose, if we wish, to become a follower of a now-dead Jesus. Following a merely historical Jesus is ruled out by the Resurrection as an option for authentically 'Christian' discipleship. The rest of the New Testament is adamant and insistent on this: discipleship means following a Risen Lord.

This means that the original followers of Jesus, who had followed him during the days of his ministry, now experienced discipleship in a new mode. Yet there were necessarily and importantly aspects of continuity between these two modes. It was, after all, the same (singular) Jesus whom they were following ('Jesus Christ is the same yesterday and today and for ever': Heb 13.8); and their belief in his risen-ness did not become the excuse or occasion suddenly to abandon a focus on his historical ministry (as if to say, 'who needs to bother with that material from his earthly life, now that we relate to the Risen Jesus directly?').[8] No, Christian discipleship is forever anchored in a following of the real historical Jesus – focused on what he truly said, who he truly was, and what he truly accomplished – but now seen as all the more important because of his Resurrection. The Gospels, despite their greater focus on Jesus' historic ministry, were composed (and eventually committed to writing) because of this conviction about his risen life; and the rest of the New Testament writings, despite their greater focus on his risen and exalted life, show an evident commitment and obedience to the unique and authoritative Teaching, Person, and Work of the Jesus who had been truly manifested 'in the flesh'.

So what does the rest of the New Testament say about discipleship – this following of the historical Jesus, now gloriously raised from the dead? Here it may be helpful to gather the New Testament writings into four groups or streams which reflect the relations they have with the theology of the four Gospels:[9]

Mark, with 1 Peter and Hebrews
Matthew, with James, Jude, and 2 Peter
Luke, with Paul
John, with 1–3 John and Revelation

A full account of biblical discipleship would need to explore what each of these four streams teaches on the matter.[10] In this book, we can only focus on the first as an example.

8 This sometimes is the implied force of some interpretations of Paul's words in 2 Cor 5.16: 'even though we once knew Christ from a human point of view, we know him no longer in that way'. Yet when Paul wished pithily to remind Timothy of the essential Christian message, he wrote: 'Remember Jesus Christ, raised from the dead, a descendant of David – that is my gospel' (2 Tim 2.8). Paul's Jesus, though risen, is securely anchored in history.
9 This schema, which is of course a vast over-simplification and based on historical reconstructions we cannot fully prove, was perhaps first suggested by Earle Ellis, who also connected it to a possible geography: Rome (Mark), Jerusalem (Matthew), the Aegean (Luke), and Ephesus (John).
10 For a preliminary exploration of discipleship in these other streams of the New Testament, see e.g. N. T Wright, Following Jesus: Biblical Reflections on Discipleship (London: SPCK: 1994, revised 2014).

1 Peter and Hebrews: one of four streams of discipleship

One of the most powerful ways to read 1 Peter is to see it as the mature reflections of the same Peter who had been discipled by Jesus – not only during those three years of historical ministry, but now also through a further thirty years of active service of the Risen Lord. The impetuous and self-reliant, even arrogant, young man has been mellowed by the Master. His instructions to his hearers – these would-be disciples who ardently love Jesus but who, unlike Peter, have never seen him in the flesh (1.8) – are full of chastened wisdom:

(a) 'prepare your minds for action; discipline yourselves; set all your hope on the grace that Jesus Christ will bring you' (1.13);

(b) 'do not be conformed to the desires that you formerly had in ignorance' (1.14);

(c) 'Now that you have purified your souls by your obedience to the truth so that you have genuine mutual love, love one another deeply from the [a pure] heart' (1.22);

(d) 'Rid yourselves ... of all malice, and all guile, insincerity ...Like newborn infants' (2.1–2);

(e) 'For the Lord's sake accept the authority of every human institution' (2.13);

(f) 'Christ also suffered for you, leaving you an example, so that you should follow in his steps' (2.21);

(g) 'have unity of spirit [mind], sympathy, love for one another, a tender heart, and a humble mind. Do not repay evil for evil or abuse for abuse' (3.8–9);

(h) 'Since ... Christ suffered in the flesh, arm yourselves also with the same intention [way of thinking]' (4.1);

(i) 'tend the flock of God that is in your charge … Do not lord it over those in your charge … but be examples to the flock' (5.2–3);

(j) 'And all of you must clothe yourselves with humility in your dealings with one another' (5.5).

Are these really the words of the same man who had rebuked Jesus for taking up his cross, and who had cut off the ear of the High Priest's servant in Gethsemane (Mk 8.31–32; Jn 18.10–11)? Yes, they are, and as such they betray the power of spending a lifetime in the school of Jesus the Master-Discipler.

Peter's own Speech, Person, and Agenda have so evidently been transformed by those of Jesus. And we too can now be transformed in our own discipleship by heeding Peter's words. In this way we begin to see how discipleship is passed on from one human being to another, from one generation to another: as a person, schooled and trained by Jesus, reveals how Jesus has changed how they speak, who they are, and what they do.

With the Letter to the Hebrews, our ignorance of the human author of this text means we that have no way of seeing how the author has been transformed as a disciple of Jesus. Yet we should still heed the urgent call to discipleship in this powerful sermon (or 'word of exhortation': 13.22). The author develops at length a picture of discipleship portrayed as a journey – whether like the Israelites travelling through the desert or like athletes racing towards the finishing-line – and he urges us not to fall out of the race but to persevere and endure to the end:

(a) 'we must pay greater to attention to what we have heard, so that we do not drift away from it' (2.1);

(b) 'Let us … make every effort to enter that rest, so that no one may fall through such disobedience as theirs' (4.11);

(c) 'Since ... we have a great high priest who passed through the heavens, Jesus, the Son of God, let us hold fast to our confession' (4.14; cf. 10.23);

(d) 'Therefore, since we are surrounded by so great a cloud of witnesses, let us also lay aside every weight and the sin that clings so closely, and let us run with perseverance the race that is set before us, looking to Jesus the pioneer and perfecter of our faith, who for the sake of the joy that was set before him endured the cross, disregarding its shame, and has taken his seat at the right hand of the throne of God' (12.1–2);

(e) 'Therefore lift your drooping hands and strengthen your weak knees ... See to it that no one fails to obtain the grace of God; that no root of bitterness springs up' (12.12, 15);

(f) 'Jesus Christ is the same yesterday and today and for ever... Let us then go to him outside the camp and bear the abuse he endured (13.8, 13).

Intriguingly, in making his appeal for perseverance in following Jesus, the writer frequently alludes to episodes from Jesus' historic life – his anguish in Gethsemane (5.7–10), his Via Dolorosa (13.13), his receiving such 'hostility ... from sinners' during his Passion (12.3). The author of Hebrews is therefore pursuing the same strategy, albeit in an epistle, as Mark pursues in his Gospel – namely using the example of the historic Jesus as the deepest call and challenge to ongoing discipleship of Jesus' followers. This is also seen in 1 Peter (2.21–25; 5.1; etc.). All three authors are saying the same:

(a) To be a disciple of Jesus means obedience to the Risen Lord through patterning our lives on the example of the historic Jesus;

(b) We must walk 'in his steps' and travel 'in the way', sharing in his suffering, trusting in his victory.

Discipleship is thus a journey, walking in the direction set by Jesus towards the place of his final vindication, while knowing that this journey is one which he has first walked himself and therefore is one along which he accompanies us with his presence. For, as Hebrews so aptly portrays him, this Jesus is simultaneously: our brother (or companion), who is now with us on the road; our pioneer, who once walked this road ahead of us; and our perfecter, who has successfully reached our shared destination in the Heavenly Jerusalem (see 2.11; 12.2, 22). He has gone ahead of us, but he has not left us behind: he is also here with us, such that, even in the darkest valleys, we are not alone.[11]

Conclusion

A full analysis of the New Testament's teaching on this theme of following Jesus would confirm what this preliminary survey has discovered: that Christian discipleship is inextricably linked with both the historical and human Jesus and the Risen and Exalted Jesus. We cannot, as it were, follow the one without the other, for these two are not separate entities, but gloriously united, as our Creeds affirm, in 'Our One Lord Jesus Christ'!

Seeing discipleship in this light and with fresh confidence in the centrality of the Resurrection, we may return in closing to the final, post-Resurrection chapters of the Gospels. In Matthew 28 we hear the Risen Lord's commission to 'make disciples'. In John 20–21 we see Jesus sending the apostles (as he was sent by the Father), restoring Peter and calling him to feed his sheep. Finally in Luke 24 we see the Risen Jesus effectively emphasizing six key themes as essential for his future disciples: his Resurrection (vv. 34, 46), his Cross (vv. 26, 46), the Holy Spirit (v. 49), the Scriptures (vv. 27, 44), the Sacrament (or breaking of bread, v. 35), and Mission (v. 48). Luke portrays these six as being the top priorities of the Risen Lord for those who want to follow in his Way. This is Jesus' curriculum for his training course in biblical discipleship; or, this is how

11 Jesus promised to be with the disciples to the end of the age, and to send them the advocate (Mt 28.20b; Jn 14.18, 23; 16.7).

to follow the Lord Jesus the way he himself intended – that is, Jesus' way.[12] It would be great if these six themes were each given their proper place within the life of our Anglican Communion. The first two focus first, appropriately, on Jesus himself; the next three explore three different streams which are to be treasured in our common life (the charismatic, evangelical, and sacramental), and the last reminds of the ultimate goal of all our discipleship – Christ's mission to his world. Perhaps we see here in Luke 24 the Risen Lord's agenda for the Anglican Communion – Jesus' way for us to be truly his disciples.

12 These six themes have been developed by Peter Walker in his book on Luke 24 and Acts 2: The Jesus Way, with foreword by J. I. Packer (Oxford: Monarch, 2007), revised 2nd edn (London: Whitchurch Publishing, 2016).

Chapter 2 – Discipleship in the Early Church

Once individuals had come to faith in Christ, how did the early Church help them to continue walking in 'the Way' (as the faith is described in Acts 19.9)?[1] How did they nurture their newborn infants? Or, to use a phrase that Luke uses to describe Paul's activity, how was it that they 'strengthened the … disciples and encouraged them to continue in the faith' (Acts 14.22)?[2]

Much of this disciple-making activity will have been done in one-to-one contexts, as individuals encouraged new or younger believers in the faith. At this distance in time we cannot now gauge the measure or content of this 'individual discipling'. Yet presumably this was happening every single day – from the very first Easter Day onwards!

Sometimes this 'individual discipling' may have become a more intentional 'mentoring'. Thus Priscilla and Aquila invited Apollos into their home 'and explained the Way of God' (Acts 18.26). Paul too, despite his wider responsibilities, may have found time to do this: he speaks of going 'from house to house' in Ephesus (Acts 20.20) and was evidently mentoring the young Timothy by writing him two encouraging letters.[3] In all such discipling by individuals there will inevitably have been the three elements noted above as the mentor shared their Words, Wisdom, and Way. It was not just about teaching but also about modelling; not only truths but practice and lifestyle. So Paul spoke frequently of mimesis

1 This is not the same question as how the New Testament Christians did their evangelism, on which see e.g. Michael Green's Evangelism in the Early Church, revised edn (Grand Rapids, MI: William B. Eerdmans, 2004).

2 Significantly Luke often uses this term 'disciples' in Acts to describe believers, transferring this title, first used of those following Jesus in Galilee, to those following the now Risen Jesus in a wider variety of places: Jerusalem (9.26), Joppa and Caesarea (9.36; 21.16), Tyre (21.4), Syrian Antioch (11.27–29; 14.26–28), Galatia (14.20–22), and Phrygia (18.23). Note too Paul's concern that they should not see themselves as disciples or 'followers' of Apollos or Paul himself but only of Jesus (1 Cor 1.12; 3.21–23).

3 Both 1 Timothy and 2 Timothy contain strong tones of personal mentoring; see also Paul's words to Timothy in e.g. Phil 2.19–22

or 'imitation' as he encouraged people to imitate his way of life.[4] And his words to the new Thessalonian believers (whom he had needed to leave after only three weeks: see Acts 17.2) give us a clear insight into what Paul would wish to see in any such 'individual discipling':

> like a nurse tenderly caring for her own children. So deeply do we care for you that we are determined to share with you not only the gospel of God but also our own selves … As you know, we dealt with each one of you like a father with his children, urging and encouraging you and pleading that you … lead a life worthy of God … (1 Thess 2.7–8, 11–12)

More obviously, there was 'corporate discipling' – when believers gathered together 'encouraging one another' (Heb 10.25). By AD 57 Christians were meeting 'On the first day of the week … to break bread' (Acts 20.7); so we see immediately the importance given both to Sunday worship and to the Sacrament. Moreover, back in Acts 2, Luke had cast a vision for Christian gatherings with a fourfold focus: the apostles' teaching, the breaking of bread, fellowship, and prayers. All four practices, as regular ingredients in their Sunday worship, would have been a key part in the Church's instinctive strategy for nurturing her young.[5]

Of particular importance for our present purpose is the first: a devotion to the apostles' teaching. This reminds us that disciple-making in the New Testament has an irreducible element of instruction: there are truths to be received and practices to be learned. It also, crucially, alerts us to the fact that, though we are, strictly, disciples of Jesus (not the apostles), the

4 See e.g. 1 Cor 11.1; Phil 4.9. Paul likewise tells Timothy that he must 'set the believers an example for in speech and conduct, in love, in faith, in purity' (1 Tim 4.11–12).

5 The term 'fellowship' (koinonia), which means 'sharing in common' or 'partnership', should not be spiritualized; this commitment clearly led to very practical consequences (see Acts 2.45; 4.34–35), including care for widows (Acts 6.1; 1 Tim 5.3–10). For examples of corporate prayer meetings, see Acts 4.23–31; 12.5; and 13.2 (which also included fasting). For the importance of 'breaking of bread', see Paul's teaching on the Lord's Supper in 1 Cor 10–11.

only way we can truly access Jesus' truth now is through the medium of his appointed apostles. We cannot follow Jesus without, as it were, following them. We need their authoritative testimony about the Risen Jesus to follow that same Jesus authentically today. To put it another way, as disciples of Jesus we need both the Gospels and the Epistles (both the words of Jesus and the words about Jesus).

So Sunday worship gatherings in the New Testament era would inevitably have included, the following, to which Paul urges Timothy to commit himself: 'the public reading of scripture ... exhorting ... preaching' (1 Tim 4.13). These weekly practices were the essential bedrock for encouraging faithful discipleship.

But did this Sunday commitment to receiving he apostles' teaching spill over onto weekdays? Were there evening classes for the newly baptized? In particular, were new converts given extended exposure to what we would call the 'Jesus-tradition' (the material now written down in the Gospels)?[6] This is entirely possible historically and would make evident sense: for how could disciples of Jesus follow Jesus without knowing his life story or what he said? To put it another way, they too needed not just the (emerging) content of the Epistles, but also the (faithfully passed on) content of the Gospels.

So we would do well to reckon seriously with a prominence being given in the New Testament period to what we now call 'catechesis' – that is, deliberate and intentional instruction in the Christian faith sustained over several months or more. Luke hints at this phenomenon when he says that Apollos had been 'instructed in the Way of the Lord' (Acts 18.25) and that Theophilus, his dedicatee, will be able to 'know the truth concerning the things about which you have been instructed' (Lk 1.4). On both

6 For the argument that Paul's converts were indeed trained in the Jesus-tradition, see e.g. David Wenham, Paul: Follower of Jesus or Founder of Christianity? (Grand Rapids, MI: William B. Eerdmans, 1995). Moreover, were there extra sessions organized for believers with leadership potential, so that they could be trained in what we would call Christian doctrine, apologetics, or hermeneutics (in their case, how to use the Old Testament in the light of Christ)?

occasions he uses the verb kateekeo ('to teach orally, often by repeating'), from which the word 'catechesis' is derived. And was this instruction solely focused on doctrine? No, Paul's firm words in Ephesians 4 make it clear that such catechesis would have involved issues of ethics, morality, and lifestyle: 'That is not the way you learned Christ! For surely you have heard about him and were taught in him, as truth is in Jesus. You were taught to put away your former way of life, your old self' (Eph 4.20–22).[7]

In conclusion, it remains difficult to be clear about the details of disciple-making in the New Testament. However, what we do know is that it was remarkably successful. Regardless of the precise details, the enterprise as a whole was evidently driven by God's Spirit. And when we ask what was their 'secret', or what was the real agent of the Church's growth, both Peter and Paul would draw attention (as Jesus himself had done in the parable of the sower, Lk 8.11–15) to the power of God's Word:

> You have been born anew... through the living and enduring word of God ... That word is the good news that was announced to you ... Like newborn infants, long for the pure, spiritual milk (1 Pet 1.23, 25b; 2:2)[8]

> And now I commend you to God and to the message of his grace, a message that is able to build you up ... (Paul in Acts 20.32)

Those closing words of Paul to the Ephesian elders at Miletus say it all. How will the Church of God not wither but grow through the testing years (and centuries) ahead? What will prevent 'disciples' from being drawn away by 'savage wolves' (Acts 20.29–30)? The answer is, always, the Word of God and his grace.

7 For a recent argument for the vital importance within Christian disciple-making of helping believers to be 'trained' in godliness and righteousness, see Tom Wright, Virtue Reborn (London: SPCK, 2010).

8 In the NIV translation, the word 'spiritual' (logikos) obscures Peter's point here. He has been speaking about the 'word' of God (logos) and now says that his readers will continue to grow by feeding on that word, as a baby feeds on milk; a better translation might thus be 'the milk of God's word'.

Intentional discipleship in the early Church

The early Church was intentional about the training of its members in living their whole daily lives in the imitation of Jesus. In the ancient Church, the normal Christian formation required of all (new) church members was primarily seen as a matter of catechesis.

Catechesis was seen as a major task of Church leaders. Many of the well-known leaders of the ancient Church set aside much time and energy for instructing new believers in the faith, in spite of their many administrative tasks.

We have many catechetical works from the ancient Church, like the *Didache* (*c.*AD 50–150), *Proof of Apostolic Preaching* by Ireneaus (*c.*AD 190), *The Apostolic Tradition* by Hippolytus, bishop in Rome (AD 170–235), and others. People interested in the Christian faith were first seriously questioned about their intentions, and then entered into a period of three years of learning.

Central to the formational teaching in catechesis were the Holy Scriptures. Proper formation in church taught people how to live and what to believe, on the basis of the Holy Scriptures.

In the ancient Church the meaning of the sacraments was taught in catechesis, not just as a preparation for participating in those sacraments, but also to make these sacraments an important part of the continued spiritual formation after people entered the Church. Every celebration of the Sacrament brought to mind the material and ethics learned during catechesis.

As soon as the Church created formal Creeds, these were used in the training of new believers. Believers had to learn the Creeds by heart and needed to have an adequate (if limited) understanding of their content and meaning. This was specifically taught in catechesis, but it was also repeated in the liturgy of the Church. In each church service this reminded the believers of the basis of their faith.

The Lord's Prayer was also part of the instruction to new believers. They would learn it by heart. Thus they were taught how to pray, and after Baptism, during the Eucharist they would pray this same prayer over and over again. What they learned during their time of initiation would be repeated weekly in church for the rest of their life.

The formal catechumenate was followed by ongoing formation. For the catechumens,[9] there was continuity between hearing the Church's teaching during their time of initiation in church services and hearing the same teachings by the same preachers in daily Mass and weekly Sunday worship services after their Baptism.

To the sermon, baptism, Eucharist, ancient creeds, and the Lord's Prayer we could add other liturgical elements like the confession of sins, the announcement of forgiveness, the readings from Holy Scripture, the members' greeting each other with the kiss of peace, etc. Weekly repetition played an important role in the formation of Christians in the ancient Church.

The liturgy was the early Church's most effective manner of Christian formation for all of its members. After the formal period of instruction, followed by Baptism, the believers were weekly taught the Christian life through the liturgy of the Church – the verbal and visual re-enactment of all the basic aspects of the Christian faith they had learned about. Through its liturgy and all aspects of it, they were taught how to be true followers of Jesus Christ.

This Christian formation – *discipleship training* – was church-based, communal, and led by Church leadership. It was not something separate for those interested in discipleship classes, but something all believers were supposed to undergo, initially in formal training, and after their Baptism through participation in the communion of the saints in the normal life of the Church.

9 The term means 'learners', from 'catechesis', 'the teaching'.

Chapter 3 – Recent Roman Catholic Theology of Disciple-Making

In the light of the emphasis currently placed by Pope Francis on 'missionary discipleship' it is appropriate to review very briefly some of the background documents and related Catholic theology emerging at the Second Vatican Council and more recently. (Given the transformative nature of the Second Vatican Council for the Roman Catholic Church, and the confines of this book, the earlier and significant Roman Catholic theology of discipleship will not be covered here.[10])

The Prologue to the Catechism of the Catholic Church begins with three simple sections in which we are reminded that:

> (a) [God] calls men and women to seek him, to know him, to love him with all his strength;
>
> (b) He invites them to become, in the Holy Spirit, his adopted children;
>
> (c) All Christ's faithful are called to hand the Gospel on by professing the faith, by living it in fraternal sharing, and by celebrating it in liturgy and prayer.[11]

This embryonic expression of holistic Christian discipleship and disciple-making, however, finds scant reflection in the body of the Catechism itself, where the word 'disciple' is almost exclusively used as a historical reference to the first followers of Jesus.

However, if we turn instead to the documents of the Second Vatican Council itself (which predate the Catechism) we find something more interesting.

10 For more background reading see Michael P. Hornsby-Smith, An Introduction to Catholic Social Thought (Cambridge: Cambridge University Press, 2006).
11 References to man and men are of course meant to be inclusive of women or simply human beings.

Gaudium et Spes famously begins with the words,

> The joys and the hopes, the griefs and the anxieties of the men of this age, especially those who are poor or in any way afflicted, these are the joys and hopes, the griefs and anxieties of the followers of Christ. Indeed, nothing genuinely human fails to raise an echo in their hearts.[12]

It set the agenda for followers (disciples) of Christ in a renewed, outward-looking, world-serving Catholic Church. Gaudium et Spes has been regarded as one of the most far-reaching of the Council documents, dealing as it does in Part 2 with so many aspects of human existence – economics, family life, armaments and peace, culture, and international development. Having discussed each of these in detail the document concludes:

> Mindful of the words of the Lord: 'By this everyone will know that you are my disciples, if you have love for one another' (Jn 13.35), Christians can yearn for nothing more ardently than to serve the [people] of this age with an ever growing generosity and success ... In this way [people] all over the world will awaken to a lively hope.'[13]

Here discipleship is clearly seen as (a) related to the whole of life and (b) a life of witness which naturally 'awakens' others.

Ten years later Paul VI published his call to Catholic evangelization Evangelii Nuntiandi, in which he firmly linked 'gathering in Jesus' with the missional vocation, saying, 'after Jesus' resurrection, the "little flock" gathers together in Jesus' name in order to seek together the Kingdom, build it up and live it.'[14] Paul VI's teaching on the missional character of Christian discipleship had a strong influence on John Paul II, who in 1990 published his own Redemptoris Missio, which has an even stronger

12 Gaudium et Spes, 1.
13 Ibid., 93 (emphasis added).
14 Evangelii Nuntiandi, 13.

focus on proclamation being linked to a life of discipleship. 'The church', it proclaims, has a 'special connection with the kingdom of God and of Christ, which she has the mission of announcing and inaugurating among all peoples.'[15]

The story reaches its fruition, for our purposes here, with the 2013 publication of Pope Francis's Evangelii Gaudium, which speaks of the Church as 'a community of missionary disciples'. He goes on: 'we can no longer think of ourselves as "disciples" and "missionaries" but always together as "missionary disciples"'.[16] In this document the life of discipleship and the vocation of disciple-making are finally locked together as one.

Beyond the official documents of the Church, Catholic missiologists such as Stephen Bevans, Robert Schroeder, Sherry Weddell, Therese D'Orsa, Mark Francis, and Anthony Gittins have increasingly focused on the missional impact of holistic discipleship, of lives lived to the glory of God through the power of the Holy Spirit. Stephen Bevans in particular has reflected on the understanding of missionary disciples and how this relates to the cultivation of a missional spirituality.

15 Redemptoris Missio, 18.
16 Evangelii Gaudium, 120.

Chapter 4 – Discipleship in the Orthodox Tradition

Discipleship as a concept is not very familiar in today's Orthodox communities, outside monastic circles. Yet it has not always been like that.

In the first three centuries of Christian history, one could trace uninterrupted lines of spiritual genealogy all the way back to the apostles of Christ. Besides being the natural way in which the apostolic kerygma was transmitted and character was formed, such authority relationships were very important, particularly at the times of persecution that dominated that period, when converts to the Christian faith were often asked to pay the supreme price for their religious decision.

The situation changed radically after the Edict of Milan (AD 313), when it suddenly became fashionable for people to be Christian. This substantially ended the disciple-making reflexes inherited from apostolic times. Yet this tradition did not disappear completely, but was perpetuated among the Desert Fathers and Mothers, who, at least initially, withdrew in monastic communities, especially in Palestine and Egypt, as a reaction to the accommodation of Christian communities to the ways of the secular world. In these early monastic communities, the Christian formation of new disciples was the duty of more mature followers of Christ (abbas and ammas), much as had happened in Christian communities in previous centuries. It was a model rooted in mystical vision and strengthened by an emphasis on ascetic practices, aimed at crucifying the passions of the flesh.

One may ask what happened to the Christian formation of those who continued to live in society. It is interesting that, as the news about the wisdom of the desert monastics reached larger Christian communities living in the world, some Christians started visiting the desert monastic communities, in search of models and sources of spiritual enrichment. This, of course, supplemented the influence of committed bishops and priests, who often paid a high price for speaking openly against those who were following the ways of the world.

This dual model of Christian discipleship dominated most of the rest of Orthodox history. In time, monastic communities became more and more influential, so that we may rightly say that discipleship in Orthodoxy is dominated by the monastic model.

A key theological concept for the Orthodox understanding and practice of discipleship is that of theosis, which sadly is often misunderstood as a claim that human beings can be deified, can become God. This is to misunderstand theosis, a powerful concept which draws on a number of biblical passages.[1] It helps us to understand that as we become more open to God, we become recipients of the life of God and begin to reflect the glory of God more faithfully. Theosis is not about a change of our essence (we remain fully human) but rather about our becoming more fully alive, more human as humanity was intended to be, because we have allowed God's life to fill and eventually overwhelm us. Discipleship takes us along this road until eventually the (human) mirror is no longer seen, but only the reflected glory of God.

The limits of this text force us to jump over centuries of significant Orthodox history in order to arrive at the present time. The mystical and ascetical model of Christian discipleship promoted by the Eastern Fathers is still the predominant one in Orthodoxy today. If our suggestion is true, one may rightly ask how this monastic vision of Christian spirituality could still respond to the needs of Orthodox believers living in secular environments. It is in response to such needs that the Institute for Orthodox Christian Studies in Cambridge has created 'The Way', a course of adult catechism similar to the Alpha course. Yet most Orthodox communities in the majority Orthodox countries have little interest in such attempts, being dominated by nostalgia for the times when they had a dominant position in society. Nevertheless, as secularism progresses, Orthodox Christians will be forced to face the challenge of re-imagining Christian discipleship in the new context, in the light of their tradition of spiritual formation.

1 See particularly 2 Pet 1.4 and 2 Cor 3.18.

Chapter 5 – History of Anglican Formation and Discipleship

The sixteenth-century English Reformation took place within a much broader European catechizing culture. The century saw the creation of foundational catechetical or/and confessional material within almost all Christian traditions: those by the Catholic Melchior Cano, by the Council of Trent, and of Luther, Heidelberg, and others. Interest in catechesis was already rising in the fifteenth century, but the widespread Christian divisions of the next century fanned the catechetical flame significantly, as different groups sought to solidify the teaching of their particular party over and against the errors of other Christians. All Christians of the era tended to see the truth as being intellectually grounded, and therefore saw the Gospel's substance as best communicated through formal teaching. The invention of state schooling in Europe at this time is tied to these dynamics. The Churches in both Protestant and Catholic regions took charge of education, supported by the civil authorities, with religious teaching at the centre.

The reformed Church of England followed a special route in these broader developments. Unlike many of their continental neighbours, the English did not institute public schooling, but instead literacy was tied directly to church catechesis, usually by the parish priest or curate. In this, England continued to follow a medieval model. But with the reformations beginning in the 1530s, this model was now governed by explicitly Protestant values of scriptural knowledge and godly learning, as can be seen in Cranmer's Preface to the English Bible of Henry VIII. Hence, although Cranmer would later maintain a very medieval (and short) catechism in his Book of Common Prayer (BCP), the assumptions regarding its use were very Protestant: that is, in teaching the Catechism (usually prior to Confirmation), Cranmer and his successors understood that the Catechism itself would be only the basis for a much broader scriptural elaboration done by the local priest, in a way that would suit a number of different audiences. The great Anglican poet-priest George Herbert testifies to this when he describes how a priest's theological literacy is based on parish catechesis:

> The country parson hath read the Fathers also, and the schoolmen, and the later writers, or a good proportion of them, out of all which he hath compiled a book and body of divinity which is the storehouse of his sermons … This body he made by way of expounding the Church Catechisme, to which all divinity may easily be reduced … Yet hath the parson, besides this laborious work, a slighter form of catechising, fitter for country people; according as his audience is, so he useth one or other, or sometimes both, if his audience be intermixed.[1]

By 1570, Alexander Nowell's semi-official *Catechism*, based on the BCP kernel, ran to several hundred pages, and England had already seen a proliferation of other printed catechisms. In all cases, these diverse catechetical elaborations shared two central features: they were scripturally embedded and tied to the vernacular Bible, and they maintained the ancient catechetical structure of Creed, Commandments, Lord's Prayer, and Sacraments. The use of this form was mandated by the BCP's own rubric until the revision of 1662:

> The curate of every parish, or some other of his appointment, shall diligently, upon Sundays and holydays, half an hour before evensong, openly in the church instruct and examine so many children of the parish sent unto him, as the time will serve, and, as he shall think convenient, in some part of this Catechism.

Over 800 different English catechisms have been identified from the sixteenth and seventeenth centuries. Millions of copies were published and distributed during this time, all witnessing to England's 'unspectacular orthodoxy' and 'undogmatic Protestantism', as one scholar has put it (Ian Green). They were used in parishes, homes, and more formal private schools, and their successful dissemination and use contributed to England becoming, by the mid-seventeenth

1 From George Herbert, A Priest to the Temple (1632; New York: Thomas Whitaker, reprinted Charleston, South Carolina: BiblioBazaar, 2009), chap. 5.

century, the most highly literate and, especially, biblically literate nation in the world.

But the Church of England's catechetical success, which propagated a widespread general Christian literacy, also led to the weakening of more particular and personal notions of faith. Already by the mid-seventeenth century, we hear of Anglican pastors decrying the way in which Puritan 'preaching hath preached away catechising'.[2] Puritan homiletic focus was meant to teach, of course; but to do so according to very specific theological outlooks and more importantly with a view of conversionary renewal. After the Civil Wars of the mid- seventeenth century and the decade-long prohibition of Prayer Book Anglicanism, Puritan conversionism was largely discredited as a Church-wide programme. The restoration of episcopal and Prayer Book Anglicanism in the 1660s also unleashed new energies in the area of mission: first, in terms of renewing local parish life, and then, in the eighteenth century, in terms of non-English Christian outreach itself. In both cases, aspects of Puritanism found their way back into the formational life of the Church of England.

It is also important to remember that in each century there were many Christian leaders who were not concerned simply to teach belief, but also to release people into active ministry to others – praying for the sick, addressing poverty, releasing the oppressed, and so on. In the sixteenth century John Baxter and in the seventeenth century John Wesley both had active ministries of prayer and healing. The seventeenth-century theologian John Owen wrote very clearly about the need for the active deployment of the gifts of the Spirit. Catechesis and the 'equipping of the saints' for practical ministry always go hand in hand.

The most important development of the late seventeenth century was the invention and establishment of religious societies throughout England. This major movement owes its origin to a German Lutheran, Anthony Horneck. The idea was to have local parish groups which met regularly, under the supervision of the priest, for prayer, Bible study, instruction,

2 Robert Shelford, Five Discourses (Cambridge: Thomas Buck and Roger Daniel, 1635), p. 75.

and charitable works. The idea caught on, and the societies proliferated around London and then in the country as a whole, influencing in turn pietist groups back in Germany. More specifically missionary societies emerged from this movement, but usually with the formational aspect or prayer and scriptural learning intact.

Among the leaders of this missionary outlook was Thomas Bray, a parish priest of enormous energy and vision for extending catechesis to parishes in Britain and in North America. He resourced local teachers, using the standard equipment of the Church: Bible, Catechism, hymnal, and other books (including his own multi-volume catechism). Bray first founded the Society for Promoting Christian Knowledge (SPCK), which sought to provide parishes and clergy with printed teaching material, in 1698; and in 1701 he helped found the Society for the Propagation of the Gospel in Foreign Parts (SPG), the Church of England's first explicitly missionary group. Bray was instrumental in the support of clergy in the colony of Maryland, which he visited, and promoted what was to become a key element in Anglican mission, that is, the lay catechist. Because of the dearth of clergy in the colonies, lay leadership inevitably became important. Bray encouraged the use of catechetical 'conferences' in the colonies, much like English religious societies; and these finally gave way to a more open movement of lay catechesis within the overseas Churches.

Bray shared his theological focus with most other renewing Anglicans of his era: he was a primitivist, in that he saw the early apostolic Church as the model for a fulfilled Christian life, and he was firm believer that the basis for the Christian life itself was the *covenant of grace* that the individual entered into in Baptism. The two areas of fervent visible witness, as well as of activist engagement, followed from this focus: Christians were called to provide a vital corporate witness within their society, and they were to engage the moral demands of God's covenant with energy. Teaching, formation, and discipleship followed from this focus. Two particular elements developed and joined this *religious society mission* in the eighteenth century, sharpening the theological focus itself: first, John Wesley's Methodist societies, deriving from the same sources as Bray's, added revivalist and organizational depth; and second was the flourishing of child-centred catechesis (e.g. by Isaac Watts).

As Anglican mission evolved, the key formational instrument of its extension emerged from this: the individual lay catechist, who became the driving medium of both teaching and renewal. Indeed, the missionary and discipling work of the catechist became worldwide Anglicanism's most enduring and influential element. The SPG and later the Church Missionary Society (CMS, founded in 1799) both deployed the catechist as their chief means of mission. It is worth quoting Henry Venn, leader of the CMS in the mid-nineteenth century, on this issue, given that his understanding of the catechist's role was something he inherited: the local catechist, raised up from within the indigenous church community, often through the Church school first established by the missionaries, would become the means by which traditional Anglican teaching would be disseminated across cultures and into unevangelized areas. Venn describes this in general:

> But in respect of an organised native community, the missionary should no longer take the lead, but exercise his influence *ab extra*, prompting and guiding the native pastors to lead their flocks, and making provision for the supply for the native church of men suited for the office of the ministry, whether catechists, pastors, or evangelists; and in this position, which will be readily ceded to him, of a counsellor of the native church, to strive to elevate its Christian life and its aggressive energy upon surrounding heathenism.[3]

Venn emphasizes the apostolic character of the catechist's work, using an image of St Paul's tent-making witness, in this discussion of a CMS mission in Ceylon:

3 William Knight, Memoir of the Rev. H. Venn (London: Longman, Green and Company, 1880), p. 287.

> More than 100,000 coolies, chiefly from South India, are congregated in these plantations: from ten to twelve native catechists labour amongst them. The whole expense of these catechists is borne by the local funds. Those native catechists are to be under your training and superintendence, and through them chiefly you must strive to quicken the spiritual life of the Christian coolies, and to induce heathen coolies to enter the fold of Christ. Your position will be very similar to that which our blessed Saviour held with the twelve Apostles, and may His Spirit be abundantly shed on you.[4]

Finally, Venn locates the catechist's own training within the ordering of the Church's theological education:

> The native teacher who approves himself 'apt to teach' is appointed to the office of a Catechist. The office of a catechist has been always recognised in the Church of Christ for evangelistic work, his function being to preach to the heathen, and to minister in congregations of converts until they are provided with a native pastor.[5]

We should note this formational order clearly: the missionary brings up the catechist (usually through the local church school), who then may become the local pastor, thus putting the missionary out of business in that place. In fact, from the early nineteenth century on, in India and Africa, and then later in the East and in the Americas, formal theological education was really focused on the catechist, who was trained locally, or then in emerging Bible training centres. Preparation for ordination was reserved only for a few, and in fact few schools were devoted to it. Although in the later nineteenth and early twentieth centuries, schools for missionary catechists were founded in Britain, most catechist training was indigenous and was supported by local diocesan funds or those from missionary societies themselves.

4 Ibid., pp. 291–2.
5 Ibid., p. 305.

What did local catechists learn, and what and how did they teach? Mostly, they first learned to read, and then they mastered the traditional elements of the Anglican catechetical programme: Bible, Creed, Commandments, and Lord's Prayer and Sacraments. These elements were taught in basic ways, using key translated texts almost exclusively (since more elaborate books could be had only in English). This scriptural and BCP-related material was digested usually in an often unconsciously adapted fashion for the local culture, and was taken by the catechists to the rural areas and villages where they lived and worked. Each catechist would share these elements with their compatriots differently. Acting as primary evangelists, they also then became congregational leaders and more formal teachers for new Christians and children preparing for Baptism. As revival-based conversion emerged in, for example, parts of eastern African in the 1920', catechists often took on the role of leaders for the Methodist-styled religious societies that structured the revival: leading prayers and hymns, confessional testimony, and Bible study.

The catechist movement was the backbone of almost all Anglican mission from the nineteenth century on, in Africa, India, North America, the Arctic, Australia, and more. (The exception was the United States, where official formation remained mostly priest-centred, except in cases of church schools.) It even involved Anglican mission to the Jews. The Bible, BCP, hymnals, and sometimes unusual books like Watts's catechisms were all translated into the vernacular and became the means for discipleship formation, adapted for use in the hands of the individual local catechist. As John Pobee writes:

> The catechist … is the unsung hero of African church history. He was often a teacher or a lesser mortal who prepared the ground for the missionary of priest, nursed the congregation, won the souls for the church, and stayed with the poor at the grassroots. He was the holy one on whom the Christian community was focused … Perhaps the record of Joseph Quashie (1900–1983), father of the Rt. Rev. Kobina Quashie, retired bishop of Cape Coast is the most profound [example …]. Though equipped with only

> elementary education, and after working as a clerk at Aboso Gold Mines, in 1936 he did a one-year catechist training at St Augustine's Theological College, Kumasi. After that Quashie nurtured a congregation at Bogoso in Western Region. In 1952 he was with the training of Catechists at Mampong, Ashanti. After that he continued to nurture congregations in Central, Western and Eastern Regions of Ghana. After retirement in 1972, he took residence at Madina, near Legon and the Anglican Church of Madina was the fruit of his evangelistic zeal.[6]

Contemporary realities within the Anglican Communion have decisively changed in the West, and are in the process of changing elsewhere. Schools are no longer places where literacy is tied to Scripture learning, let along church formation in general; the BCP no longer has much common currency; catechesis as a foundational ordering of Christian life has few common tools to use. Hence,

(a) There is increased reliance on worship as formation, but with the dissolution of the BCP's unified usage, there has been a demise of common worship and regularity; hence worship's formational capacities have been weakened;

(b) There has been an increased reliance on revival techniques, through the media-driven influence of American evangelicalism, and these have entered into the centre of worship, but there has been no comparable deployment of catechesis;

(c) Indeed, catechesis has all but disappeared in the West as a formal and central element of life;

(d) Bible study remains, along with some small group elements, but with little common or formal connection to the church's common life.

6 John S. Pobee, The Anglican Story in Ghana: From Mission Beginnings to Province of Ghana (Kaneshie-Accra: African Books Collective, Amanza Ltd, 2009), pp. 224–30.

By contrast, we have seen a renewed interest in Anglican catechesis, with the Global South catechesis project and other similar initiatives in the Anglican Communion. These mark a new recognition of the loss of Anglicanism's catechetical focus, but still await significant institutional integration within the Churches of the Communion.

Chapter 6 – The Five Marks of Mission

> As Anglicans, we value the 'five marks of mission', which begin with the preaching of the Gospel and call to personal conversion, but which embrace the whole of life.[1]

The Five Marks of Mission were first developed as four marks by the sixth Anglican Consultative Council meeting (ACC-6) in Badagry, Nigeria, in 1984.

A fifth mark was added in 1990 by ACC-8, after it had appreciated the missiological and biblical implications of the creation and the evident environmental crisis that humanity and the whole created order was facing, which needed a Christian response. In adopting the new fifth mark of mission, ACC-8 stated, at its meeting in Wales, that 'We now feel that our understanding of the ecological crisis, and indeed of the threats to the unity of all creation, mean that we have to add a fifth affirmation.'[2]

The Five Marks of Mission are not only a significant expression of a common Anglican Communion statement about mission but are also an important expression of the Communion's (w)holistic understanding of God's mission.

By definition the mission of the Triune God is holistic, for it has at its heart the whole of creation, the human and non-human creation, and understands the totality of the human as having physical, emotional, psychological, social, and spiritual aspects.

1 Lambeth Indaba: Capturing Conversations and Reflections from the Lambeth Conference 2008. Equipping Bishops for Mission and Strengthening Anglican Identity, The Lambeth Conference, pp. 8–9.

2 Mission in a Broken World: Report of ACC-8, Wales 1990 (London: Church House Publishing, 1990), p. 101. The Five Marks of Mission are: to proclaim the Good News of the Kingdom; to teach, baptizes, and nurture new believers; to respond to human need by loving service; to seek to transform unjust structures of society, to challenge violence of every kind, and to pursue peace and reconciliation; to strive to safeguard the integrity of creation and sustain and renew the life of the earth. See more details about the Five Marks of Mission and other associated resources at: www.aco.org/identity/marks-of-mission.aspx.

Mission therefore is 'God's way of loving and saving the world',[3] and at the heart of this mission is the 'the movement of God's love toward people [and the rest of creation]',[4] in which 'The Church [the whole Body of Christ] as an instrument for mission' has been called to participate. Therefore, God's mission is at the very heart of the life and existence of the Church and Christian service and ministry.

The biblical narrative in which the Five Marks of Mission are anchored begins with the creation, where humanity is the climax, but this is followed by relationships breaking down: between human and God, between humans themselves, and between humans and the rest of the creation. The narrative, however, ends with relationships restored in and by the life, ministry, and death of Jesus Christ.

As the life and ministry of Christ were to bring about healing, wholeness, and reconciliation of God's creation (human and non-human), the Five Marks of Mission express both the reconciling and the healing nature of God's mission.

The Anglican Communion's understanding of mission is guided by the belief that God's unconditional love is for all, and therefore the Church works with diverse groups of people in a way that respects and protects their intrinsic human dignity and value as God's children regardless of their ethnicity, faith, social or political status, etc.

The Five Marks are therefore grounded in and shaped by this understanding of God's holistic and integral mission. Anglicans strive to 'proclaim the Good News of the Kingdom' in word and action by fostering 'response to human need by loving service, by seeking to transform unjust structures of society and striving to safeguard the integrity of creation and sustain and renew the life of the earth.'

3 The Official Report of the Lambeth Conference 1998: Transformation and Renewal, July 18–August 9, 1998 (Harrisburg, PA: Morehouse, 1999), p. 121.

4 Lambeth Indaba, p. 8.

The Five Marks of Mission demonstrate that God's mission is much deeper and wider than is sometimes understood and show that the mission of God is often (if not always) integral, contextual, personal, local, national, and global – an essential reality of our world today!

In this sense, 'the Five Marks of Mission can be described as a DNA of God's holistic and integral mission, in that while each mark is complete in itself, it is nevertheless an important part of the whole and contributes to the whole'.[5]

Although not every Anglican or Episcopalian is aware of the Five Marks of Mission, it is probably the only well-known statement on mission issued by and for the Anglican Communion and used fairly widely within the Communion and among other denominations.

The Five Marks of Mission are a model for inclusive ministry, and a useful tool. They are not perfect nor complete definition of mission, but an important basis for a holistic approach to mission. A number of Anglican provinces and dioceses have developed resources based on the Marks of Mission that are used in equipping members to live out these marks in their context as an expression of their faith. Resources include Bible study, Lent reflections, prayers, liturgical worship material, materials for community engagement, and advocacy.

Revealed in the Five Marks is the reality that mission is lived out in the everyday life of a baptized follower of Christ in obedience and in response to Christ's call to be witnesses to the Kingdom of God in the world.

5 Cathy Ross (ed.), Life-Widening Mission: Global Anglican Perspectives (Oxford: Regnum Books, 2012), p. 147.

Chapter 7 Healing and Discipleship

For each disciple of Christ, there is a personal and transforming exploration of what it means to be a human person, brought into being by God and growing into the likeness of his Son, Jesus Christ. The Christian understanding of healing and wholeness is a unique aspect of our faith: it offers insight into God's mission and ministry in this world for all time. The objectives of this ministry reach to the furthest boundaries of human experience as expressed in 1990, by the World Council of Churches, which described health as:

> a dynamic state of well-being of the individual and society, of physical, mental, spiritual, economic, political and social well-being – of being in harmony with each other, with the material environment and with God.[1]

In the year 2000, at Pentecost, the report A Time to Heal was published on behalf of the House of Bishops of the Church of England and circulated to all Primates in the Anglican Communion. The report sets out the state of the healing ministry at the beginning of the third millennium and offers extensive recommendations for the development of this ministry and its full integration into the life of Christian communities. In the report the healing ministry is defined as:

> **Visionary** – because it beckons us towards the future and a glimpse of the kingdom – the hope of creation renewed in perfect health and wholeness.
>
> **Prophetic** – because it calls us to reconsider our relationships with God, each other and the world and to seek forgiveness and a new start in our lives.

1 file:///C:/Users/Johnk/Downloads/2.CTH_definitions_and_glossary_13.6.2007.pdf, and also see A Time to Heal: The Development of Good Practice in the Healing Ministry. A Hand Book (London: Church House Publishing, 2000) p. 377.

> **Dynamic** – because Jesus Christ is with us to the end of time. When we pray for his help, he comforts, strengthens and heals us, responding to our deepest needs.[2]

This deeper understanding of Christ's healing ministry expresses God's ultimate aim for all of his creation and his desire for our growth into holiness and wholeness beyond this human lifespan, through the blessings of faith, hope, and love, into eternal life in his Kingdom. Healing in this way transcends sin and death, as Jesus shows us the Way through his own death, Resurrection, and Ascension.

While suffering, sickness, and broken relationships are universally shared characteristics of human existence, the offer of reconciliation and healing through the love, compassion, and mercy of God is also set in chronological time. Thus, a deepening of understanding with regard to holistic healing and the well-being of all of God's creation is central to contemporary and emerging forms of discipleship: it is the fertile ground on which Christian faith and discipleship can be built, in such a way that it engages with the whole human condition: past, present, and future.

Learning to understand this and to live out the Gospel in today's world involves integrating and expressing God's healing and reconciliation in our own lives and making them possible in the lives of those around us. This way of living faith transcends all boundaries: every aspect of discipleship and of service in the name of our Lord should embody healing and reconciliation, for ourselves, for each other, and for God's creation. One of the most profound challenges and opportunities for the Church today is to foster this understanding of the Gospel and to enable God's people to live it out in daily lives.

Resolution 8 ('The Church's Ministry of Healing)' of the 1978 Lambeth Conference affirmed and underscored the ministry of healing in the Anglican Communion, and stated thus:

2 A Time to Heal; see the back page of the book.

The Conference praises God for the renewal of the ministry of healing within the Churches in recent times and reaffirms:

(1) that the healing of the sick in his name is as much a part of the proclamation of the Kingdom as the preaching of the good news of Jesus Christ;

(2) that to neglect this aspect of ministry is to diminish our part in Christ's total redemptive activity;

(3) that the ministry to the sick should be an essential element in any revision of the liturgy (see the Report of the Lambeth Conference of 1958, p.2.92).[3]

Resolution 73 of the 1930 Lambeth Conference was emphatic not only on the need for spiritual preparation before participating in healing sessions but also on collaboration with those involved in medical professions, because healing is to do with the whole person or wholeness:

Resolution 73 – The Ministry of the Church – The Ministry of Healing

(a) The Conference commends to the Church 'The Ministry of Healing' (SPCK, 1924), being the Report of a Committee set up in accordance with Resolution 63 of the Lambeth Conference of 1920.

(b) Methods of spiritual healing, such as unction or the laying-on of hands, should be used only in close conjunction with prayer and spiritual preparation.

(c) There is urgent need for co-operation between clergy and doctors

3 All Lambeth Conference resolutions can be found on the Anglican Communion website at: www.anglicancommunion.org/structures/instruments-of-communion/lambeth-conference.aspx.

since spiritual and physical treatment are complementary and equally necessary for true wellbeing.

(d) Seeing that the ministry of the Church is a ministry for the whole man, it is of the utmost importance that the clergy should equip themselves for a fuller understanding of the intimate connection between moral and spiritual disorders and mental and physical ills.

The Instruments of Communion have made similar statements and resolutions in commending to the Churches of the Communion the importance of exercising healing ministry as an essential element of the proclamation of the Gospel and God's Kingdom.[4]

Deliverance ministry as mission and ministry

Eight of the twenty-seven healings recorded in the Gospels are associated with exorcism and deliverance, and they include occasions when Jesus commanded unclean and harmful spirits to leave the people they afflicted.[5]

Deliverance ministry is a key dimension of mission and ministry. Of all the broad range of ministries to which disciples of Christ are called, deliverance is noteworthy as having been given by Jesus Christ (Mt 10.1–16; Mk 3.13–19, 6.13; Lk 9.1–2). It is integral to the commission given by Jesus Christ to the disciples who would become the twelve apostles: to preach and teach about the Kingdom of God as the Good News, or the Gospel, to heal the sick, and to cast out demons.

4 Also see ACC-6, Resolution 16, 'Ministry of Healing': 'In preparation for Lambeth 1988 the Council recommends that serious consideration be given to the role of the healing ministry in Scripture, together with its actual functioning, relevance and potential importance in today's Church and its mission.' Bonds of Affection: Proceedings of ACC-6, Badagry, Nigeria, 1984 (London: Anglican Consultative Council, 1984). All ACC resolutions can be found on the Anglican Communion website at: www.anglicancommunion.org/structures/instruments-of-communion/acc/acc-6.aspx.

5 A Time to Heal, pp. 167, 170, 171.

However, the ministry of deliverance and exorcism is not an all-member ministry: it is a distinct feature of apostolic ministry entrusted to those with whom the Bishop chooses to share it. **While every Christian can and should engage in prayer for deliverance from evil, the Lord's Prayer being the most well-known prayer, not every Christian is called by God or by the Bishop to be an exorcist.**[6]

Deliverance has been defined as:

> release from evil spiritual influences which oppress a person or hinder the individual's response to God's saving grace. Prayer by an individual or group of Christians for a person who, it is believed, is being troubled by evil.[7]

The prime objective of deliverance ministry is to deliver the person seeking help through this ministry into a personal relationship with our Lord Jesus Christ. It is a ministry of pastoral care, the Word, and prayer and sacrament, and is inextricably linked to discipleship, spiritual formation, and growth into wholeness.

The ministry of deliverance and exorcism has not ceased to be part of the Lord's commission: it is an essential aspect of episcopal ministry within the life of the Church today.

Deliverance from evil and concerns about paranormal issues affect people across all walks of life, of every age group, gender, race, economic situation, and ethnicity. Some people who seek help from the Church have little or no experience of Church membership or have left the Church for various reasons. Often they have tried to find answers to their concerns or questions through other sources before approaching the Church. Consequently it is fundamentally important to recognize that each case

6 The Principles of Canon Law Common to the Churches of the Anglican Communion (London: Anglican Consultative Council, 2008), www.anglicancommunion.org/media/124862/AC-Principles-of-Canon-Law.pdf (see Principle 78).

7 A Time to Heal, p. 337.

is unique, as each person is unique, in order to understand the context and background and to respect the individuals involved.

An important challenge in deliverance ministry, therefore – which is also a precious opportunity to teach about the Good News of the Gospel – is to help the person concerned sift through the ideas and beliefs they have acquired in their search, to discern spiritually what is Christian and compatible with Christian teaching and what is not, what is of God and what is not.

Every case has a past and present context and involves individual and shared hopes and fears for the future. Many of the problems are connected with 'life issues', including a person's perception of mortality and death, their experience of life and world-view, and their search for reassuring answers to the big questions about what lies beyond. Essentially the deliverance ministry is a significant portal through which the Church can reach out and preach the Gospel into contemporary society and make disciples.

When the person affected approaches the local church or parish priest, the first few moments of contact with the Church tends to shape their perception of whether the Church cares about them and has anything to offer them that is relevant to their current situation.

A high proportion of those seeking help have other problems too, including physical and mental health issues and problems with relationships, which may influence their spiritual distress: thus a multi-disciplinary approach using the resources of healthcare is recommended. Because genuine cases of demonic possession are so rare, they must be carefully determined through diagnosis and discernment of distinct symptoms to avoid inappropriate ministry.

Consequently deliverance is best done at local level with, as far as possible, the goodwill and practical involvement of the parish priest. A safe and effective strategy for deliverance ministry within the Church which realizes its potential for mission and ministry therefore should be multi-layered and multi-disciplinary and linked with other aspects of the life of the Church at every level. Deliverance ministry should be done in the context of continual pastoral care within the local Christian community.

Experience shows that those who receive help through the Church's deliverance ministry tend to remember the quality of pastoral response provided. This approach highlights the need for parish priests to be trained and equipped to provide spiritual counsel and nurture within the concept of whole-person care.

One of the great challenges for the Church today is to express and to teach the love of God in a context where suffering, sickness, and mortality are universal characteristics of human existence and can drive individuals and communities to look for answers, advice, help, and deliverance from practitioners, belief systems, organizations, and commercial enterprises beyond the Church. In this context, ministries such as deliverance and healing, exercised as part of the holistic pastoral ministry of the Church, serve God's purposes in his world and give us signs of his Kingdom coming now.

Healing discipleship is both a pastoral response to the expressed needs of the communities among which we live and minister and a bold proclamation of the Good News of salvation in Christ which heralds a new creation in which all will know wholeness, health, and well-being.

Chapter 8 Discipleship and the Instruments of Anglican Communion

The Anglican Communion, through the Instruments of Communion,[1] has always recognized that at the heart of Christian faith and living is the call of the whole people of God to witness to Christ as we follow him in daily life both as individual Christians and as the community of faith; and in the power of the Holy Spirit to be light and salt in our front-line areas in society.

The statements and resolutions of the Lambeth Conference and the Anglican Consultative Council (ACC) have particularly spoken powerfully, since they were established, to this Gospel imperative and reality of Christian calling to be disciples and disciple-makers.

This review explores some of the themes that have emerged from reading the statements and resolutions of the Instruments of Communion.

Baptism and ministry

Baptism is seen as the primary mark and sign of our Christian identity, allegiance, and commitment to pattern our lives on the life, ministry, and teaching of Jesus Christ. The 1998 Lambeth Conference report asserts that 'Baptism … is the foundation of all Christian ministry', and that 'Through Baptism, each follower of Christ is called into that ministry and the Holy Spirit gives the gifts necessary to carry it out.'[2]

The report also points out that:

1 Instruments of Communion are formal structures that are a symbol of unity; they are: the Lambeth Conference (a meeting of all bishops every ten years or so), the Anglican Consultative Council (which is similar but not exactly equivalent to a synodical body and meets every three years), the Primates' Meeting (of heads of churches called and chaired by the Archbishop of Canterbury), and the Archbishop of Canterbury (as the President of the Anglican Consultative Council and chair of the Lambeth Conference and focus for unity in the Communion).

2 The Official Report of the Lambeth Conference 1998, p. 192.

> By their baptism, all the members of the laos as Body of Christ commit themselves to its ministry in the world. This ministry may take place within their context of family or household, the village, neighbourhood or community, the school, workplace or arena of civil authority, and through volunteer service. It is not limited by age, education, social status or any other criterion.[3]

The report makes it clear that while Baptism opens one to a particular way of living, and will bring varied gifts to the Body of Christ, it does not mean that the baptized person is automatically equipped; thus

> All the baptized are to be equipped to perform their ministries in accordance with their gifts and 'to give a reason for the hope that is in us' (1 Pet 3.15). . . . All Christians who would respond faithfully to their baptism deserve and need continuous formation in the biblical story, the faith of the Church, the ways in which the values of God's reign shape our living, the practice of prayer, as koinonia with God, the church's worship and its call to serve the world.[4]

The Holy Spirit and the whole people of God

The centrality of the teaching ministry of the Church runs as a recurring theme through the texts of many Lambeth Conference reports, with emphasis on equipping the whole people of God (the Body of Christ) – all the baptized, lay, clergy, and bishops need lifelong formation and equipping.

3 Ibid., p. 193.
4 Ibid.

The 1998 Lambeth Conference report affirmed

> the deepening understanding of the relationship between baptism and the ministry of the whole people of God; as well as the complementary relationship between the ordained and lay ministry. [5]

It must be emphasized here that the Anglican Communion statements make it very clear that discipleship is not merely to do with 'teaching' but rather that 'equipping' involves the 'doing' or 'service' as one lives the implications of one's faith in Christ. Thus, the bishops at 1948 Lambeth Conference stated, 'we believe that Christians generally are called by God to take their part in the life of the world, and through the power of God's grace to transform it'[6].

Here as in other statements and resolutions, the significance of disciples being 'empowered' by the Holy Spirit in their ministry and service is crucial, just as it was with Jesus Christ himself as well as the apostles and the early Church. The 1988 Lambeth Conference would thus acknowledge

> that God through the Holy Spirit is bringing about a revolution in terms of the total ministry of all the baptized ... enriching the Church and making Christ known to men and women as the hope of the world.[7]

Resolution 7 ('The Holy Spirit and the Church') of 1978 is candid in acknowledging the central role of the power of the Holy Spirit in Christian witness and calling all Anglicans to a new openness to the outpouring power when it states:

5 Ibid., p. 202.
6 Resolution 40 ('The Church and the Modern World – The Christian Way of Life') of the 1948 Lambeth Conference.
7 Resolution 45 ('Mission and Ministry of the Whole Church') of the 1988 Lambeth Conference.

(1) The Conference rejoices at the abundant evidence from many parts of the world that there is renewed awareness of the power and gifts of God's Holy Spirit to cleanse, sustain, empower, and build up the Body of Christ.

(2) We have seen increased instances of parish life being renewed, of individual ministries becoming effective agencies of God's power to heal and reconcile, of witness to the faith and proclamation of the Gospel with converting power, and of a deeper involvement in the sacramental life of the Church.

(3) We rejoice at the prompting of God's Spirit within the many expressions of ecumenity among Christians, for the new forms of Christian communal life springing up and for Christian witness on behalf of world peace and the affirmation of freedom and human dignity.

(4) The Conference, therefore, recalls the entire Anglican Communion to a new openness to the power of the Holy Spirit; and offers the following guidance to the Church, in the light of the several ways this Spirit-filled activity may be best understood and represented in the life of the parish.

(a) We all should share fully and faithfully in the balanced corporate and sacramental life of the local parish church. Informal services of prayer and praise need this enrichment in the same way as the sacramental life needs the enrichment of informal prayer and praise.

(b) We all should ensure that reading and meditation of the Bible be part of the normal life of the parish and be accompanied by appropriate study of scholarly background material so that the Scripture is understood in its proper context. Those who search to understand the scholarly background material in their reading of the Bible should ensure that they do so under the guidance of the Holy Spirit, so that the Scripture is understood in its proper context.

(c) We all should search out ways to identify with those who suffer and are poor, and be involved personally in efforts to bring them justice, liberation, healing, and new life in Christ.

(d) We should remember always that the power of the Spirit is not to be presented as either an exemption from suffering or a guarantee of success in this life. The road from Palm Sunday to Pentecost must pass through Good Friday and Easter. It is at the cross that new life through the Holy Spirit is found, and in the shadow of the cross that Christians must pray 'Come, Holy Spirit.'

The above references show the determination of Anglican leaders to ensuring the Anglican Communion is committed to the biblical vision and call for whole life discipleship for the whole people of God serving the whole world (together) under the empowerment of the Holy Spirit.

To this end the Anglican Communion recognized the need to be specific about the kind of equipping necessary for the whole people of God – laity and clergy.

With regard to **bishops**, Resolution 39 of the Lambeth Conference 1968 affirmed that they 'should have opportunities of training for their office'.[8]

Resolution 9.2 ('Stewardship') of the 1978 Lambeth Conference speaks specifically about lifestyle issues, saying:

> In the opinion of the Conference, the scriptural injunction 'he who would be chief among you, let him be the servant of all' requires bishops to reject pretentious life-styles and

8 Resolution 39 ('The Episcopate') of the 1968 Lambeth Conference and the report of ACC-1, Time is Now: Anglican Consultative Council First Meeting, Limuru, Kenya, 23 February – 5 March 1971 (London: SPCK, 1971).

> by example to lead their clergy and people in the wise use of personal resources and also those of the Church.

These resolutions underscored the need for leaders, as disciples of Jesus, to be models of Christian life and living in every sphere of life.

With respect to the equipping of the **clergy**, apart from the prerequisite theological formation for ordination, Resolution 42 of the 1968 Lambeth Conference urged

> the dioceses to provide continuing training for the clergy after ordination, and to relate the programme of study to the new situations and developments presented by a rapidly changing world.

The other significant category that both Instruments of Communion have laboured much about is the laity. Recalling Baptism as the primary basis for Christian living, Resolution 25 ('Ministry – The Laity') of the 1968 Lambeth Conference recommended that

> each province and regional Church be asked to explore the theology of baptism and confirmation in relation to the need to commission the laity for their task in the world.

And the text report of the 1968 Lambeth Conference is emphatic in stating that

> The ministry, the service, of the Church to the world is and must be discharged mainly by the laity ... The ministry of the laity does not consist solely in service to the Church or in the Church's worship. It also demands witness to the Christian gospel through word and deed in the world ... In the home, at work, in industrial disputes, in the exercise of economic power whether as employers or as employed

> … it is for the laity to bring to bear Christian influence towards social justice, compassion, and peace.[9]

However, it is not enough to expect laypeople to live their faith in every sphere of their influence without dully equipping them for that task. Therefore, Resolution 27 of the same Conference observed that 'there is an urgent need for increase in the quantity and quality of training for laypeople for their task in the world.'

Even more comprehensive is Resolution 125 of the 1958 Lambeth Conference, 'The Family in Contemporary Society – The Duties of the Laity', which states:

> The Conference rejoices that, more and more, lay men and women are finding their true Christian ministry in their daily work in the world, as well as in the organised life of the Church … The clergy need to understand this, and to help, by their teaching and by sharing in the thoughts and problems of the laity in their daily work, to deepen this ministry. The laity need equally to understand it, to help one another by Christian discussion and loyal comradeship to bear a better witness, and to offer in their work both their responsible, skilled gifts, and a deeper understanding of the Christian faith about God and man.

A number of important strands are contained in this resolution and deserve further exploration. This and other resolutions consider work and other human activities as a form of vocation.[10]

9 The Lambeth Conference 1968: Resolutions and Reports (London: SPCK and New York: Seabury, 1968), p. 24. All Lambeth Conference resolutions can be found on the Anglican Communion website at: www.aco.org/structures/instruments-of-communion/lambeth-conference.aspx.

10 See Resolution 72 ('Progress in the Anglican Communion Missionary Appeal') of the 1958 Lambeth Conference, which states, 'The Conference urges that men and women ready to devote themselves to Christian literary work, including journalism, should be enlisted and trained to regard such work as true vocation in the service of the Church.'

Resolution 22 ('The Church and the Modern World – The Church and the Modern State') of the 1948 Lambeth Conference is emphatic in calling

> all Church members to find their incentive to work, not only in security and gain, but chiefly in service and good workmanship, as an offering to the glory of God.

The report of the 1998 Lambeth Conference makes this observation:

> The Church is most faithful to its calling when all its members recognise their vocation as disciples of Christ and that they received their vocation in baptism, whatever form of ministry they might exercise. It is important that this be emphasised in our baptismal preparation and liturgies.[11]

The Lambeth Conference of 1998 called for the

> need to develop and strengthen models of adult catechetical practice ... which stress both God's grace and the full demands of the Gospel as [new believers] accept and practice a new way of life.[12]

The wholistic formation of **children and young people** features prominently in the Anglican Communion texts. There is appreciation of the value of children and young people as full members of the Church and human family. Resolution II.8, 'Young People', of the 1998 Lambeth Conference acknowledged

> their definite value in the human family. They are for us in the church, as they were for Jesus, signs of the Kingdom of God among us. Their presence and ministry in the church is essential for the whole family of God to be complete.

11 The Official Report of the Lambeth Conference 1998, p. 192.

12 Ibid., p. 193.

In the same resolution, the bishops committed themselves to 'give leadership in their diocese, to ensure that the church is safe, healthy, and spiritually enriching community for children and young people' and that 'Christian young people are equipped ... for service in the Church and community ... in leadership skills and to exercise that leadership in the life and mission of the church.'[13]

Various avenues have been identified through which the Church's teaching ministry can enhance the holistic development and role of children and young people in the world as they grow in their faith as followers of Jesus. These areas include, among others, the following four:

Schools

Schools, colleges, and universities, particularly those with a Christian ethos, have been hailed for their 'unique value for the community' in fostering holistic development of children and young people. To this end Resolution 29 ('The Church and the Modern World – Education') of the 1948 Lambeth Conference asserts that the opportunities that 'Church education' provides for children's 'religious, moral, and social training' should be made open 'to all who desire them.'

Meanwhile, Resolution 32 of the same Conference states:

> The Conference welcomes the steps taken in some universities to make provision for courses designed to give general instruction in Christian faith and practice to those who are not students in theology. It also urges that a chapel of corporate worship should be provided in every university and university college.

Resolution 18 of the 1908 Lambeth Conference called upon the Anglican Churches 'to promote and cultivate the spiritual life of students in secondary schools and universities', whereas Resolution 11 of the same Conference observed with concern that

13 Ibid., Resolution II.8, parts i, iii, and v.

> purely secular systems of education are educationally as well as morally unsound, since they fail to co-ordinate the training of the whole nature of the child, and necessarily leave many children deficient in a most important factor for that formation of character which is the principal aim of education.

Sunday school

Resolution 30 ('The Church in the Modern World – Education') of the 1948 Lambeth Conference 'emphasised the responsibility of individual clergymen and parishes in the work of Christian education' and acknowledged 'a deep debt of gratitude [owed] to the Sunday and day school teachers and youth leaders' for advancing the 'Church's teaching ministry to children and young people with devoted service'.

Resolution 14 of the 1908 Lambeth Conference called for

> the need to strengthen Sunday school system … [and identify] best methods of improving Sunday school instruction, and … right relations between Sunday schools and the various systems of catechizing in church.

Home and family

The Anglican Communion takes seriously the role of parents in holistic child development, and thus Resolution 19 of the 1908 Lambeth Conference expressed a desire

> to lay special stress on the duty of parents in all conditions of social life to take personal part in the religious instruction of their own children, and to show active interest in the religious instruction which the children receive at school.

Resolution 122 ('The Family in Contemporary Society – The Christian Family') of the 1958 Lambeth Conference even goes further in spelling out the practical ways in which the Christian family could be a solution to the challenges faced by society and family; it states:

> The Conference believes that a most important answer to the crushing impact of secularism on the family life lies in a return to the discipline of prayer and in a faithful common Christian life in the household. It urges that the clergy work towards this end by teaching both the privilege and the means of such worship, and of Bible reading, in which fathers should take their due place with mothers and children as members of and ministers of a worshipping community.

It is worth noting that the Communion has not treated youth as purely 'recipients' of service of adults from the Church but that children and young people are an important mark of the Church.

Today's reality is such that children and young people below the age of 35 form the majority of the Anglican Communion, and in countries such as those in the sub-Saharan Africa, over 60 per cent of the population are below 35 years. So the importance of equipping and building capacity of young people in society, and particularly in church, must not even be a matter for discussion.

Modern technology

In the light of today's technological advancement and social media, it is important to note what the Anglican Instruments have previously said. With regard to media, the 1948 Lambeth Conference recognized the influence of films and expressed some anxiety,[14] whereas at the next Lambeth Conference, Resolution 62 ('Progress in the Anglican Communion Missionary Appeal') asked that

> every opportunity be taken, at the local and provincial level, to make effective use of such channels of communication as television, radio, films, religious drama, and the secular and religious press;

a point which today would equally apply to the internet and social media.

The 1948 Lambeth Conference had in fact asked for 'further investigation and experiment on the part of the Church in film production and radio programmes as a means of religious and missionary education, and full co-operation with experts in the field'.[15]

Scripture

The centrality of Scripture in the Anglican Communion is a key part of Anglican identity and has been promoted by the Instruments of Communion as central to Anglican discipleship. Resolution 6 ('The Bible') of the 1958 Lambeth Conference acknowledged 'with gratitude the dominant place which the Anglican Communion has always given to the Holy Scriptures in its public worship. It welcomes … the close relation of the word and sacrament'.

14 Resolution 34, 'The Church and the Modern World – Education', of the Lambeth Conference 1948 stated, 'Recognising the great influence of films and broadcasting both for good and for evil, we welcome the efforts now being made to improve their quality; sharing the anxiety of many of teachers and education authorities lest the films shown to children should undermine sound educational influences, we particularly welcome the provision of wholesome films and broadcasts for children.'

15 Resolution 35, 'The Church and the Modern World – Education', Lambeth Conference 1948.

There was a call to find imaginative and sensitive ways to present the Bible, such as using 'all the resources of literature, art, music, and drama, and of new techniques appealing to the eye as well as to the ear'.[16]

The Conference invited 'the Churches of the Anglican Communion to engage in a special effort during the next ten years to extend the scope and deepen the quality of personal and corporate study of the Bible,'[17] and also 'called on Church people to re-establish the habit of Bible reading at home, and commend[ed] the growing practice of group Bible study'.[18]

16 Resolution 10, 'The Bible', Lambeth Conference 1958.
17 Ibid., Resolution 12, 'The Bible'.
18 Ibid., Resolutions 12 and 5, 'The Bible'. Also see Resolution III.1 ('The Bible') of the 1998 Lambeth Conference, which invited all provinces to 'to promote at every level biblical study programmes which can inform and nourish the life of dioceses, congregations, seminaries, communities, and members of all ages'. The Official Report of the Lambeth Conference 1998, p. 394.

Stewardship

One other recurring theme in the Lambeth Conference resolutions is the emphasis on stewardship – teaching and practice – as part of Christian life and living. Stewardship is to be seen primarily as a response in obedience to God's call to care for the environment, which is first and foremost located in the creation narrative. To this end, the 1968 Lambeth Conference would urge 'all Christians … [to] take all possible action to ensure man's responsible stewardship over nature; in particular in his relationship with animals, and with regard to the conservation of the soil, and the prevention of the pollution of air, soil, and ocean'.[19]

The responsibility to care also relates to the way and purpose for which personal (and corporate) resources are expended and the importance of sustaining the Good News of the Kingdom to the glory of God using the gifts and skills that God, the creator, provides. Resolution 64 ('Progress in the Anglican Communion Missionary Appeal') of the 1958 Lambeth Conference therefore urged all

> Church people to the duty and privilege of stewardship, of which sacrificial, planned, and systematic giving is part, to the end of the souls of the people may be enriched, and the needs of the Church met, including the adequate support of its ministry and provision for the extension of its work.

Giving both oneself and one's resources is expected of one who is a follower of Jesus.

19 Resolution 6, 'Man's Stewardship of Nature', Lambeth Conference 1968.

Prayer and worship

Worship is central to the life of Anglicans and Episcopalians, and public worship or shared worship is especially important for a community of faith as the gathered people of faith. The gathered community brings with it 'the joys and sorrows of our varied everyday lives. When we open ourselves to God in worship, our eyes are opened to God's ways in the world and we are empowered for service and mission.'[20]

Worship is a time when Christians deepen their personal and corporate relationship with God and are energized for God's mission in their day-to-day lives. In fact the word 'Mass', which many Anglicans use for Eucharist or Holy Communion, is from a Latin word, missa, which means dismissal or sending forth.

It is therefore a fitting common practice in many Anglican Church liturgies around the Communion to send forth worshippers at the end of a church service to 'Go in peace to love and serve the Lord' – to live out God's love and mission from Monday through to Sunday. This is a great way to end and to send forth Christians to embody and participate in the holistic mission of God as they live their discipleship in every situation of their lives through to the next Sunday.

The life of 'prayer and study', both individual and corporate, is affirmed and encouraged, as well as recognizing the importance of creating opportunities for deepening of spiritual life – mind and heart – for both lay and clergy. Resolution 71 ('Call to Prayer') of the 1988 Lambeth Conference, for example, called

> upon individuals, prayers groups, congregations, devotional organizations, and religious communities to give renewed emphasis to the work of prayer … call[ing] the bishops of the Anglican Communion to give a strong lead in the

20 Stephen Pickard and Duleep De Chickera, The Anglican Way: Signposts on a Common Journey, Signposts Series, 1 (London: Anglican Communion Office, July 2008), p. 9.

> ministry of prayer in all its forms, so that we may know God's will for our time and be empowered for the mission of the Lord Jesus Christ.

The second ACC report, Partners in Mission, on the 1973 meeting in Dublin, observed that 'without the renewal of the Church both spiritually and structurally, its evangelism [and witness] cannot be effective'.[21]

The most recent and major resolution made on discipleship comes from the 1998 Lambeth Conference (Resolution III.22), and sums it all up:

> This Conference –
>
> (a) affirms our trust in the power of God's Spirit to ensure that all persons are made full disciples and equally members of the Body of Christ and the people or *laos* of God, by their baptism;
>
> (b) while recognising the necessity of the ordained ministry and special responsibilities which are given to various members of the Body, also recognises that all the baptised share in the common priesthood of the Church;
>
> (c) notes that the life, practice, polity and liturgy of churches everywhere should exemplify this understanding of our community and common life; and
>
> (d) affirms that in baptism all are called to personal commitment to Jesus Christ and should be given education and opportunity for ministries which include worship, witness, service and acts of forgiveness and reconciliation in the setting of their daily life and work.

21 Partners in Mission: Anglican Consultative Council, Second Meeting, Dublin, Ireland, 17–27 July 1973 (London: SPCK, 1973), p. 47.

Conclusion

The above review of the Anglican Communion statements shows an unequivocal emphasis on, and the need to be intentional in, planning and provision for equipping the whole people of God for ministry in the world – the object of God's love.[22]

The Lambeth 1998 report asserts that 'unless Christians are encouraged corporately "to go to school" with Christ, to be nourished by teaching and sacraments, and to grow up into his likeness (Eph. 4:11–16)' they cannot bear fruits of discipleship.[23] As such 'the Church is a school in which the gift of teaching is acknowledged, but in which all the teachers are themselves learners'; and 'the Church [is] to be a teaching community not simply for its own sake, but for the sake of its mission to the world'.[24]

The report also affirms that

> The Church is commanded to go to all nations and make them disciples of the Lord (Matt. 28:19f). His followers are sent by Christ into the world, as he was sent by the Father into the world (John 17). God has entrusted the Church's ministers with the task of being ambassadors, and makes an appeal for reconciliation through them (2 Cor. 5:18f.).[25]

It means that

The Church's life is never wholly private. Because Christian mission and ministry are carried out within the context of a given society, therefore the ways the Church is related to its society are of crucial importance for the mission and ministry.

22 Jn 3.16, 17.
23 The Official Report of the Lambeth Conference 1998, p. 43.
24 Ibid.
25 Ibid.

In this sense, Christian life and living (or wholistic discipleship) is the DNA of what it means for Christians to be followers of Jesus and sent by him to be his ambassadors and witnesses in God's world.

It makes sense to end this section with a resolution that is probably the most comprehensive and candid in calling Anglicans to relate their faith to their everyday life, quoted here in full: Resolution 37 ('The Church and the Modern World – The Church Militant') of 1948:

> The Conference urges all Church people to look upon their membership of Christ in Church as the central fact in their lives. They should regard themselves as individually sharing responsibility for the corporate life and witness of the Church in places where they live. They should discharge this responsibility and give a distinctive witness
>
> (a) by the regularity of their attendance at public worship and especially at the Holy Communion;
>
> (b) by the practice of private prayer, Bible reading, and self-discipline;
>
> (c) by bringing the teaching and example of Christ into their everyday lives;
>
> (d) by the boldness of their spoken witness to their faith in Christ;
>
> (e) by personal service to Church and community;
>
> (f) by the offering of money, according to their means, for the support of the work of the Church, at home and overseas
>
> Thus there will be in every locality a living centre of Christian faith, witness, and fellowship.

Part B

Contemporary Anglican Praxis of Discipleship

Introduction

This second part of the book gathers a selection of case studies and descriptions of contemporary disciple-making and discipleship from around the world and seeks to encourage the need to learn from others and to share our own experiences and insights. Examples here of discipleship and disciple-making, as much as possible, cover a wider geographical area and a wider range of theological traditions of the Anglican Communion but evidently not every part has been covered. It is hoped that those who will engage with this book will fill these gaps.

Chapter 9 – Africa

Rooted in Jesus: an African example of discipleship and disciple-making

There is a growing consensus within the worldwide Church that discipleship is one of the key issues of our times; it is all too easy to see what happens when we lose sight of the Great Commission to make disciples of all peoples, to baptize and teach them, to pass on to them everything which Jesus passed on to us. In Africa the single word 'Rwanda' offers a chilling reminder of what happens when people are welcomed but not discipled; in a Western European context steady Church decline bears witness to an eroded and over-intellectualized understanding of discipleship. It's time for a fresh approach.

Jesus called people to follow him, to grow into his likeness, and to do the works that he did; and he called them to do this not as individuals but as a new and living community, bound together by love and united by an outward, missional focus. Christian discipleship is best understood as a form of apprenticeship undertaken in an intentional community: it is practical and corporate, and involves the whole of life. It is not to be confused with theological education; discipleship is not about what we know, but about who we are becoming.

In much of Africa this is a pressing issue. Africa does not suffer from the individualism or the pseudo-scientific scepticism which is so rife in the West; the pressures are brought by poverty, political instability, tribal ties, religious conflict, and a shortage of trained leaders and resources. With the right strategies and support, Africa is however proving to be fertile ground for discipleship, and in many ways sets an example to the rest of the world of what can happen when God moves among his people.

The Diocese of Niassa in northern Mozambique has experienced remarkable growth in recent years. The diocese's vision is 'to become a communion of communities in Jesus, through the establishment of small groups studying, discipling one another, church planting and rooting, growing in faith and changed lives together'. They have sought to teach and empower more people by training leaders to train others, to offer new life through healing and development, to facilitate new rootedness for believers and new belonging for communities. They have adopted various strategies and resources, among which is Rooted in Jesus (RinJ),[26] which forms the basis for their ministry and mission training; by 2013 they estimated there were up to 12,000 members of RinJ groups across the diocese, with each group exercising a holistic ministry to the community, including caring for orphans, supporting the sick, and providing water access and health education. 'Our church', Helen Van Koevering commented, 'is reading the Bible differently.'

RinJ was first devised in 2002 in partnership between the Diocese of Leicester (UK) and the Diocese of Mount Kilimanjaro (Tanzania), for use in a Tanzanian context where many come to faith but where educational levels are low and trained leaders in short supply. Based on Matthew 28.18-20 and 2 Timothy 2.2, it is a practical, interactive small group discipleship programme designed to help ordinary people, of any educational level, to follow Jesus in all aspects of their lives – to be everything, in both word and deed, that Jesus invited his first disciples to be. Completed over two years, it facilitates the active participation of each member of the group through the empowering presence of the Holy Spirit, so that together they may be strengthened in faith, built up into the Body of Christ, and equipped for ministry to others. The material is absorbed and practised orally, and only the group leader needs to be able to read and write. Each session is summarized by a memory verse, and members receive certificates when the group completes each of the four books of the course.

Today, the Diocese of Mount Kilimanjaro in Tanzania has a strong church-planting strategy. People are ready to give their lives to Christ; the challenge is how to disciple them and form them into living Christian communities. For many years teams have travelled to remote villages, showing the Jesus Film, inviting people to make a commitment

26 See below.

to Christ, and planting new churches; the current rate is fifty churches per year. Bishop Stanley Hotay is clear that God spoke to him from Matthew 28.18–20 of the need to make 'not converts but disciples', and commissioned the RinJ programme; the new believers are prepared for Confirmation using RinJ, new evangelists are trained and appointed, and pastors are encouraged to use the programme within their churches.

In many areas of Africa churches are becoming increasingly aware of the need to disciple children, a growing proportion of the population who are conventionally looked after in large classes by untrained Sunday school teachers; this need is particularly pressing in areas where thoroughgoing religious education is provided for Muslim children through the madrasahs. In the Diocese of Masasi, Tanzania, and the Quality Discipleship Church network, Uganda, children are being taught with RinJ Junior not simply to know the Bible stories but to pray for themselves and for one another, to depend daily on God, to share their faith with their friends. Numbers of children attending church have greatly increased, and children now play an active part in ministry within their communities.

The Gospel writers show that following Jesus cannot be reduced to a single dimension; as disciples we are called to move beyond our individual identities and become a 'a community modelling and ministering an imperfect foretaste of the new heaven and the new earth'.[27] This is happening in many ways in many places across Africa, where increasingly people are realizing that we are called not just to follow Jesus but to follow him together, and to do so in context-dependent ways. In each of the examples above, the starting point has been different; in each place, discipleship has been woven in unique God-given colours into the same pre-existing fabric of community. In these models from Africa, discipleship is not a matter of individual study or devotion, but a call for the entire Christian community to do something new together. A church is a community of disciples responding to God.[28]

27 Graham Cray, 'Remembering the Main Thing', Fresh Expressions Bulletin, September 2013.
28 See Alison Morgan, Following Jesus: The Plural of Disciple is Church (Wells: ReSource, 2015).

The role of schools in the discipleship of children and young people in Kenya

The Gospel story is a great treasure that has been entrusted to us, and everybody needs to hear it. Effective sharing of the Gospel story with young people in schools and beyond cannot be over-emphasized for the African population, which is mostly young. In Kenya, 80 per cent of the population is under 35 years, with slightly below 60 per cent attending primary or secondary school, college, or university.

The Church (both Anglican and other denominations) has a stake in the raising of Christian children and young people through programmes at denominationally run schools and in partnership with interdenominational Christian organizations. The latter, in their student ministry, discipleship material and programmes, focus on equipping students for Christian life, for ministry and leadership within their institutions and beyond. The intention is to bring up maturing believers who are Spirit-led and Christ-centred in life, mission, and purpose. This population is also at a learning environment stage and peak, when training and equipping is appreciated. The children and young people are receptive to biblical expositions, Bible studies, and practical exercises of sharing faith both verbally and in community social outreaches such as visits to hospitals and homes for children, the aged and the disadvantaged.

The above practice does not replace the significance of the Christian home and the role for spiritual formation of the children's and youth ministry within the Anglican Church structure and setting. If this is well integrated and coordinated with what goes on in the institutions of learning the results and gains are awesome.

Networks and partnerships

The Body of Christ has many parts and one Spirit and runs beyond the individual Church as a denominational entity. There are interdenominational or Christian institutions that specialize in developing discipleship resource materials for different age groups, such as the International Fellowship of Evangelical Students (IFES) and Fellowship of Christian Unions (FOCUS), Scripture Union, Bible Society, Life Ministry and Campus Crusade for Christ, the Navigators, Child Evangelism International, and Kenya Student Christian Fellowship (KSCF), among others.

The above groups in their ministry and Bible study materials, in collaboration with the Church, seek to minister, equip, and empower the Christians of specific age brackets to know Christ and to effectively model him among their peers and beyond. Using their materials and partnering with them as developers and experts in their usage avoids unnecessary duplication while at the same time it is healthy for the Body of Christ.

The Anglican Church of Kenya is in partnership with these bodies, which supply the resources and bring in their personnel to train children and youth workers and teachers. For instance, during the Provincial children's, youth, and teachers' conferences key persons from these bodies are invited to run Bible studies, wherein delegates are put in clusters under the tutorship of the organization that has expertise for that group. The primary pupils are handled by Scripture Union, secondary students by KSCF, and university students by FOCUS, while working youth and young parents are handled by the Bible Society together with the conference facilitators and associates. When it comes to evangelism and witnessing, Life Ministry does an excellent job.

Chapter 10 – Asia

Discipleship training in Malaysia

In 2009, the Diocese of West Malaysia, seeing much growth in terms of numbers of members and churches over the past two decades, decided to return to intentional discipleship in order to encourage wholesome Christian living and the consolidation of Christian witness and spiritual formation. The Diocesan Bishop, the Most Revd Ng Moon Hing, reports:

> We have decided not to re-invent the wheel. So we went around shopping for good, workable and practical models. We came across SaRang Presbyterian Church in Seoul, [South] Korea. They have been doing discipleship training for the past 30+ years and their church has grown from nine people to tens of thousands in this period (60,000 in 2009 and now more than 100,000). As we drew closer to their type of discipleship training (DT), we realized and told ourselves that it is biblical, doable, and easy to learn. We have decided to adopt the SaRang model with slight adaptation to our local needs. Immediately churches were encouraged to start DT. As usual some were reluctant and a few were quick to embark on it. Today after six years of DT, many churches have launched it. The Malaysian Methodist, Lutheran, and Presbyterian Churches have also joined in the fray with this SaRang DT model.

To date, one of the few successful churches doing DT is Our Saviour's Church, which is situated in a nearby village in Kuala Lumpur. When the DT first started, the church had an attendance of about seventy regulars, with only the pastor and a few laypeople doing all the ministries. Today this church has raised up the largest number of people to serve as church workers and priests. Some are in the seminary while some are already serving. The present congregation of about 120 has almost everyone into DT classes and other leadership training classes, from the very senior to the children in Sunday school. The Sunday school curriculum has been adjusted and adapted into DT. Revd Jacob Bau, who is the vicar, is going around helping other churches to start DT while all the DT classes in his own church are being carried out by lay leaders. We can see life transformation among the members who have gone through the DT classes. The classes are just to spur understanding and commitment; the real discipleship begins after the classes, especially with members' daily lives in schools, offices, factories, and careers.

The DT classes stress a fivefold discipleship of life commitment, namely:

(a) Disciple of the Gospel of Christ – each to learn to master and to articulate the whole Gospel.

(b) Disciple of the Word of God – each to learn to read the Bible and to feed himself spiritually.

(c) Disciple of the Life of Prayer – each to learn to pray and to listen to God through contemplation and spiritual disciplines.

(d) Disciple of Service – each to offer some months or years to serve God in a certain capacity within the Church or society.

(e) Disciple of Mission – each to make at least one mission trip per annum outside his comfort zone.

There is no compulsion in the DT classes. Each person is allowed to develop according to his or her own pace. So far, we have seen great improvement in the church giving, serving, commitment, punctuality, walking the second mile, mission awareness, boldness in evangelism and witnessing, life change, attitude change, and willingness to serve, and we have seen people love the Word of God more, love God even more, etc.

Every September since 2012, the diocese has organized a 'Seminar for Disciple-Makers'. This is to cater for newcomers to the idea of DT and those who are interested in becoming disciple-makers. We believe that only disciples can make disciples. 'Disciples are made, not born' – this is the title of a book by Walter Henrichsen. The process of one becoming like Christ should lead to the end product, i.e. disciples, and nothing else. Churches should be assemblies of disciples of Christ and not pew-warming believers. All sermons should be discipleship-driven and should not entertain spectators with feel-good sensation. Christ's death is costly, and it would be considered worthy if he knew that his life was laid down for people who become his disciples. It would be sad for him if he knew that it is for pew-warmer believers. A disciple of Christ will ask, 'What and how shall I serve and live for Christ?' A pew-warmer believer will ask, 'What will Christ do for me?'

The diocese believes that the only way forward for Christians in Malaysia, especially with the increasing challenges of extremism, is discipleship training and making disciples faithfully.

Anglican Vitality in Hong Kong

In Hong Kong the Anglican Church has a campaign for Anglican vitality which it calls Be a 3 Stars Anglican. The Church describes this focus on discipleship as follows:

Aim: The idea of 3 Stars Anglican comes from the three stars on the Hong Kong Identity Card, which represents a full-status citizen. This campaign aims at leading Anglicans to be vital and devout disciples and to live in faith firmly every day. Through the training programme, Anglicans are trained in nine different areas. Participants have to fulfil the requirements in each category for a six-month period.

The scope of this programme includes the following features:

(a) Bible study: read the Bible at least five times a week and write a reflection about the message from God;

(b) Prayer: pray every day and create a prayer;

(c) Worship: attend Sunday services every week;

(d) Study: join a study group for at least ten hours;

(e) Care and concern: care for a friend intensively;

(f) Evangelism: share the Gospel to at least one person;

(g) Offering: increase the amount of money offering by 8 per cent;

(h) Serving: take part in at least one volunteer work;

(i) Fellowship: join a church group/fellowship regularly.

The Middle East – a reflection from a bishop in North Africa

I am thinking that many of the 'below-the-belt' illustrations and/or implications of Jesus interacting with people occurred at the margins or 'points of no return' in the cultures of his day. He, a Jewish male, deliberately initiates a conversation with a Samaritan woman, offering to put her water jar to his lips (Jn 4). To Jewish experts in Torah, Jesus chooses to put forward a Samaritan as best illustration of what it means to love one's neighbour (Lk 10.25–37). Later, he picks a real-life Samaritan to illustrate what it means to be a true lover of God (Lk 17.11–19). For a people locked in a colonial world, Jesus announces that the best bit of faith he has come across to date belongs to a Roman centurion (Mt 8.10). Within a culture that functions by saving face, that works by giving people the answer you think they want to hear, Jesus asks the parabolic question about two sons commanded by their father to work in his vineyard – one said 'No' but did; the other said 'Yes' but didn't – which was the true son to his father (Mt 21.28–32)? At the margins come the provocations that illustrate how much or how little a person or a culture or a religion may be like God. When Jesus is the potential 'disciple-maker', the provocations are well stated and more than compensated for in the manner in which Jesus comes to woo and win human beings to the love of God.

> 'Disciple-making' often carries a different connotation when the disciple-maker is someone like me! It is so easy

for me to see the 'non-scriptural' markers in someone else's life or religion or culture. Often in situations where Muslims from hierarchical, shame-oriented backgrounds become followers of Jesus, 'discipleship' quickly becomes measured by standards of Western 'honesty' or 'dishonesty', respect for punctuality, etc. Many disciple-makers among Muslims will have tales to tell of how new believers from a Muslim background have helped themselves to their belongings or their money – blissfully unaware that the sharing of resources (time and possessions) is normal and unquestioned in families and close friendship groups in many cultures. The idea that, within the family of God, time should be divided into 'private time' and 'meetings time' or money claimed as a private rather than a shared possession would be unthinkable within many cultures of the world. As a result, disciple-making becomes hung up on helping the new believer to live and pray and sing in a manner that says 'true disciple' in the mores of the disciple-maker's culture or background or church.

Intentional disciple-making has to be as much an adventure for the 'disciple-maker' as for the 'disciple' – because, for all of us, becoming a disciple is about character formation. It is about discovering where the Spirit of God applauds the norms of our culture, where he accepts some norms as a fair enough starting point and where he says 'not good enough!' about them. How to discern what he is saying? More and more, the epistles follow Jesus in raising questions about internal attitudes rather than external behaviours. Yes, we males manage, by the grace of God, not to contaminate our Christian lives by fornication or adultery, but then God wants to know what we think we are doing looking at a woman wrongly! How on earth do we get to 'be angry and sin not'?! Am I supposed to be learning at my age that 'love covers a multitude of sins'?

New believers are often pretty good at smelling out hypocrisy. Isn't it best to begin with the truth – it's not about me making a disciple out of him/her/them, but both/all of us sharing in growing in grace? I have been reading my way through several books with a new believer over the past few years. We have looked at Paul Tournier's *The Strong and the Weak*, Watchman Nee's *The God of Abraham, Isaac, and Jacob*, and M. Scott Peck's *The Road Less Travelled* as well as Gospels and Old Testament prophets. In both our lives, different questions come up. Sometimes, mine is a place of some experience (both in terms of grey hair and in terms of Christian 'maturity'); often the 'disciple's' is the place of uncomfortable wrestling with 'norms' underlying received behaviour and how God looks on that (not 'mine' to judge!). Equally, and uncomfortably for me, many aspects of the disciple's culture more closely reflect norms being valued in biblical visions: bonds of family, purity, honouring of older people, sharing of wealth, generous hosting, loyalty to the wisdom of the past. The disciple-making has to be a 'both ... and' experience to be true. It is about formation of character as much as or more than theological education; trying to reflect biblically, Christianly, on life. Something to be done, in front of Jesus, together.

Chapter 11 – Europe

Discipleship in the Diocese in Europe

Christian discipleship and formation is lifelong and continuous and calls the whole Church to be part of a pilgrimage of prayer, learning through the study of Scripture, listening, teaching, and living out the Good News as witnesses and ambassadors of Christ. In essence we are called to bring about the transformation of self and community, and this is a calling for all Christians, lay and ordained. As Anglican Christians we are informed by our particular understanding of faith, as exemplified in Scripture, Tradition, and Reason, and being part of the worldwide Anglican Communion implies that we are committed to living out the Five Marks of Mission within often multi-layered cultures in terms of country, language, and tradition.

As an example, it is not unusual for members of Anglican churches in Europe to speak one language at home, another at work, and a third at church (as is the situation, for instance, for many of our African members).

Discipleship as Anglicans in Europe has particular implications in terms of language, culture, and ethnicity, requiring an openness to engage with cultural diversity, transcending linguistic barriers, and reflecting ecumenical sensitivity.

Discipleship in Europe is marked by special blessings and challenges:

(a) That our witness and ministry take place within the particular context of being guests yet offering hospitality.

(b) That we are committed to Ecumenism at all levels, not least through our Agreements with other Churches, such as Porvoo and Meissen.

(c) That Anglicans often worship in churches and buildings graciously shared with us by those of other Confessions.

(d) That in Europe we are part of a minority Church present within larger faith communities and Churches, in some places where the majority of the population belong to one denomination (Lutherans in Scandinavia, Orthodox in Greece).

(e) That we live and pray alongside people of other Christian traditions and of other faiths, such as the Muslim communities in Turkey and the ancient Jewish communities throughout Europe, not forgetting that many of the countries in which we worship were at war and occupied less than a century ago.

(f) That the diocese (of the Church of England) to which we belong covers a vast geographic territory and is characterized by diverse political, social, and economic realities.

Growing discipleship in Europe has to be considered in this context and requires flexibility of approach and willingness to explore different ways of reaching, resourcing, and sustaining God's people. It is rooted in the local chaplaincy (parish) and supported by a broad diocesan programme of teaching courses, conferences, and workshops on a variety of topics including mission, theology, pastoral care, worship, and conflict resolution.

Over the last several years, there has been an ever-increasing call for training for both lay and ordained ministry in the Diocese in Europe, and the candidates reflect the cultural and ethnic diversity of the diocese. Licensed Readers, lay theologians of the Church, are engaged in teaching, preaching, and leading worship, often supported by Congregational Worship Leaders, who are trained locally by their chaplain to assist clergy and Readers specifically in leading worship.

In addition to local and diocesan teaching resources and initiatives, Anglicans in Europe benefit from enriching opportunities offered by our ecumenical partners, through continental educational institutions, churches, and religious communities, as well as resources offered in the wider Church of England, such as the Pilgrim Course and the annual Lent and Advent courses.

Until recently an online Christian discipleship course, Foundations21, was widely used in this diocese, where vast distances necessitate the reliance on electronic communication. As this course has now been discontinued, the diocese is exploring other suitable possibilities.

Given the great diversity of Anglican congregations in Europe, the styles of worship and prayer and the particular emphasis on the study of Scripture vary considerably. Developing and facilitating discipleship is as important in the long-established expatriate English speaking congregation in France as it is in the more recent Sudanese Anglican congregation in northern Finland, or in the just-established multicultural congregation in Morocco. The ways in which discipleship is developed and deepened reflects the different background and context of the local Anglican communities. It is an ongoing challenge and opportunity to meet the needs of the particular Anglican communities in ways that are of meaning and relevance to their expression of faith. In fact, the ACC document The Bible in the Life of the Church resonates with the diverse circumstances of continental Europe.[29]

Although most services in Anglican churches in Europe are in English, there is an emerging interest in local language ministry. A particular example of discipleship coming to fruition has been the teaching and nurturing of Turkish-speaking Anglicans, which eventually led to the establishing of a Turkish-speaking congregation in Istanbul.

Christian discipleship requires us to respond to the needs among us, wherever the Body of Christ is impaired. In Europe this is exemplified on a diocesan level in such initiatives as the Campaign against Human Trafficking, where the Anglican and Roman Catholic Churches work closely together, and in the diocesan initiative to foster a greater awareness of environmental issues.

But Christian witness and discipleship can be found on many levels across the continent of Europe and include local initiatives such as the

29 Martyn Percy, Clare Amos, and Ian Markham (eds.), The Bible in the Life of the Church (Norwich: Canterbury Press, 2014).

collaboration of the Chaplaincy in Athens with other churches of that area in ministering to the vast number of illegal immigrants reaching Greek shores, and to the victims of the devastating economic crisis in Greece, providing close to a thousand meals on a daily basis. Another example of Christian discipleship lived out where need is encountered is the people of the Chaplaincy in Yerevan, Armenia, who offer support to the very great influx of Syrian refugees, many from the ancient Christian communities of the Middle East, fleeing into Armenia from the terrible circumstances of the war in Syria.

Christian discipleship in Europe is inevitably interwoven with a profound sense of its complex history, acute challenges, and need for blessing.

Chapter 12 – The Americas

Community and mission in Latin America and the Caribbean

Discipleship in the Latin American and the Caribbean (LAC) is marked by the need of loving service for big, deep, lasting, and inclusive transformation.

Latin America is a formerly colonized region with long history of violence of all kinds and hope, resilience, and resistance, all at the same time. It is a continent marked by Christianity with sword and genocide but at the same time by love and sense of service and community. It is a colourful region where difference is the norm and where religion is very much an inherent part of existence.

Discipleship is a deep requirement undertaken by Jesus. Jesus, God incarnated, through his presence, word, and actions, got the attention of a large audience. As a result of the context in which we live, and driven by the call from Christ to baptize and transform the world, it is imperative to understand discipleship in a sense of a continuous process of changing, adapting, and transforming. Violence (especially against women and children), crime, poverty, xenophobia, forced migration, climate change, deforestation, and their results affect the majority of people in the region, and religious intolerance and inequality flow like a river. The churches have chosen the path of love, dialogue, and compassion, organizing communities, and making more disciples as a way of facing these challenges.

Following the example set by Jesus, churches in LAC are fostering disciples as a key part of fulfilling the call not to be 'conformed to this world, but be transformed by the renewing of your minds, so that you may discern what is the will of God – what is good and acceptable and perfect' (Rom 12.2), always having in mind that the religion that pleases God is the path to 'Wash yourselves; make yourselves clean; remove the evil of your doings from before my eyes; cease to do evil, learn to do good; seek justice, rescue the oppressed, defend the orphan, plead for the widow' (Isa 1.16–17).

All this for the glory of God:

> Thus says the Lord: Do not let the wise boast in their wisdom, do not let the mighty boast in their might, do not let the wealthy boast in their wealth; but let those who boast boast in this, that they understand and know me, that I am the Lord; I act with steadfast love, justice, and righteousness in the earth, for in these things I delight, says the Lord. (Jer 9.23–24)

In this process of discipleship, it is very important to pay attention to the method, the way, the path, and the language (not only idiom). The children of God (all equally brothers and sisters) must have

> the same mind … in you that was in Christ Jesus, who, though he was in the form of God, did not regard equality with God as something to be exploited, but emptied himself, taking the form of a slave, being born in human likeness. And being found in human form, he humbled himself and become obedient to the point of death – even death on a cross. (Phil 2.5–8)

A crucial theological concept held by churches in LAC, and a key life experience for believers, is that God always takes the initiative and comes to meet us; he delivers us himself, because God is love and compassionate (1 Jn 4.19; Hos 1–3, 11). God's gift of himself is unconditional in a twofold sense: he does not set conditions, nor does he accept constraints.

Many churches in LAC are developing ways of making disciples for the Kingdom of God by empowering people and communities to strive for transformation of inequality and violence. The Diocese of Honduras, for instance, has developed an educational programme and family gardening project, gathering people from poor communities and covering themes like the Bible, leadership, ecclesiastical management, and Anglican identity, as well as helping them to develop better and sustainable techniques for family farming or gardening and climate awareness by not using chemicals on land. One important key feature here is taking the initiative and making church present where the need is, where the most vulnerable require love and service (diaconia).

The story of the couple on the road to Emmaus (Cleophas and probably his wife Mary) in Luke's Gospel (Lk 24.13–35) is actually a teaching on how to make disciples and change realities. Most churches in LAC strive, with great success and joy, to embody a pattern of discipleship that is inspired by Luke's story and explained as follows.

Responding to those in need

Moving out of one's comfort zone and taking the initiative to be where people's needs are is a requirement to be disciple. Following Jesus is demanding but rewarding. In Honduras the Church is placing itself in places where community and development are required.

Matching the pace

This involves paying attention to the community and people's reality by journeying together in their context and rhythm of life, being careful not to trespass. Company is key on the journey. In Guatemala, through the 'Savings with Education Program', the Church is helping people learn how to save money, manage their own business, and support others in the process.

Being interested in and aware of the local context

When churches establish training initiatives for discipleship the first question is 'What are you discussing with each other while you walk along?' (Lk 24.17). A big part of discipleship is to understand the context of both church and people, and how they are influenced. Being part of one Communion is very helpful in exchanging experiences and information to foster deeper and lasting disciples for the Kingdom of God.

Being ready to be silent and listen

Discipleship requires silence in order to listen to each other deeply. The methods of training always include integrated spaces for mutual listening and dialogue. This is a good way of listening to what God is revealing to his people. Transformation, peace, and reconciliation are achieved through true processes of silence, dialogue, and mutual listening. The Anglican Church of Brazil organizes retreats for leaders during the year to strengthen their capacity of dialogue with each other and the society.

Reading the Bible TOGETHER

Reading the Bible together and doing theology for transformation are another key point in Luke's story, when Jesus offers the two disciples a new perspective on the nature and mission of the Messiah. Imprisoned as they were in and by the ideo-theology of the Roman Empire (the dominant force that wanted uniformity and to silence people) and of comfortable, corrupted religion, Jesus offers them new insight about the promised Messiah. And he does so by starting with the things they already knew, but had forgotten, or had been 'prevented from understanding' by the dominant ideo-theology. They had been waiting for someone else to solve their problem.

Many people were trained in this passive expectation from the cradle. Someone, more powerful, more educated, more mature, and with more experience, would lead them and solve their problems. Here, it is not simply a question of reading, studying, and interpreting Scripture, but of asking: which interpretation, to what end, using which texts? Is Jesus the Good News for everyone? These are issues that the churches in LAC struggle with when using the Bible and articulating theology, which of which they hold in high esteem. All training initiatives cover the Bible and theology as important topics to be dealt with. Theology and Bible study are always important instruments that enable discipleship to bring the glory of God and his Kingdom to bear.

Hospitality

Establishing safe and welcoming places is an essential part of Christian spirituality, and discipleship takes this matter seriously, particularly in the hostile world with its intolerance and violence. As intolerance, racism, and sexism increase in LAC, churches are preparing Christ's disciples to act differently. Jesus called disciples to build and organize missionary (eccentric) communities. Hospitality is crucial to the spirituality of many religions. When hospitality is lacking, bad things happen: just look at Sodom and Gomorrah. A vast range of Bible studies confirm this.

So the disciples do what their faith compels them to do: they invite the stranger into their home, to share their table. This is especially important in LAC, where multiculturalism is experienced and yet the indigenous peoples and Afro descendants are discriminated against and excluded.

Jesus (still unrecognized) and the couple had already shared the journey, the sadness, the doubts and discoveries (learning and unlearning). Now the disciples decided to be faithful to their faith and shared their table and their house. The gestures of welcome – and the gesture of Jesus – finally helped them to open their eyes. Here, 'opening their eyes' is a metaphor for understanding and obeying (listening within) their faith.

The clear purpose of sharing (understanding more deeply and analysing) context, reading the Bible together, and sharing the table (building community) is to collaborate, in order to create a space of hospitality, solidarity, and commitment: to life, to the path (the way of living), and to people (and nature). The LAC churches help their members become committed to the community, to love and sustain the service but also to strengthen stewardship, peace, and reconciliation, and to a life of justice, against unjust structures of society and church.

Say good words and doing good actions

Paul in his First Letter to the Corinthians, when reprimanding the community about the way they gathered to celebrate communion, recalled that 'many of you are weak and ill, and some have died' (1 Cor 11.30) because members of the community 'eat and drink without discerning the body' (1 Cor 11.29).

All provinces in LAC are very concerned to join the work for justice and peace and are reminded in Eucharistic celebration that they need each other to do so, and that the good words must be accompanied by good actions. This includes sharing our lives and resources to strength our hearts for the journey.

Sharing context

It is important to realize that sharing context and reading the Bible and worship TOGETHER are a sign of discipleship. We are known as disciples in the mission and in love to each other and to the world.

Most of the churches in LAC are working hard to turn violence of any kind, inequality, poverty, sadness, disconnection, depression, individualism, fear, and the inability to recognize the love of Jesus (and Jesus himself) at the start of the walk to Emmaus (our daily walk, journey) into an Easter pilgrimage and to arrive (all of us) at the Eucharistic table. How is it feasible to realize that the way to Resurrection is possible only when we accept to return to Jerusalem – to community, joy, dynamism, but also to the conflicts, to the Cross, in our lives, and not flee from it? The fourth-century Church Father Evagrius Ponticus, taking up the reflection of the Johannine community, said that the way to encounter and recognize God is to first encounter oneself (our purest, barest truth) and not the other – that is the road to love God and our brothers and sisters (1 Jn). The training and strategic plans from the provinces in LAC have this clear objective.

After Emmaus, the sad men and women (disciples) courageously got back on their feet and returned to Jerusalem: to the conflicts, to the crises. They returned to rebuild another possible world, full of new relationships. The dark night of the people becomes the dawn of resurrection: 'even the darkness is not dark to you; the night is as bright as the day, for darkness is as light to you' (Ps 139.12).

Called to be disciples and apostles in a changing world and Church: a North American perspective

Bishop Ian Douglas writes out of the context of North America to remind us that scholars and advocates of the missional church movement (those who advocate that the Body of Christ should be primarily about participating in the mission on God in the world and not maintenance of an institution) point out that the Church in Western industrialized nations is living at the end of Christendom. Christendom is the all-encompassing social, political, cultural, and economic system that presupposes that the Church is central to the life of a people and nation, but all of this is changing as the United States becomes both increasingly secular and multi-religious. We cannot pretend that the age that placed the Church at the centre of our public and private lives is alive and well. People are no longer flocking to church on a Sunday morning because it is the right thing to do, no matter how attractive we try to make our worship and programmes. Business as usual is not working.

Randy Ferebee, in his book Cultivating the Missional Church: New Soil for Growing Vestries and Leaders, competently describes the changing contours of the Church as we confront the realities of post-Christendom. He says that if the Church is to have a future in the post-Christendom world it needs to move: from the centre to the margin, from majority to minority status, from being settlers to sojourners, from privilege to plurality, from an emphasis on control to witness, from maintenance to mission, and from being an institution to being a movement.[30] These are aspirational goals that are not easy for those of us who have grown up in the twentieth-century Church of North America to come to terms with.

The Church as we have known it in North America must adapt in the wake of the end of Christendom or it will die. The stories we have told ourselves about what it means to be a Christian, the 'narratives of the Eurotribal church' as described by missional church thinker Alan Roxburgh, need to be reworked. We can no longer rest in our European

30 Randy Ferebee, Cultivating the Missional Church: New Soil for Growing Vestries and Leaders (New York: Morehouse Publishing, 2012).

colonial legacy as the established Church. We need a new narrative of who we are as the Body of Christ after Christendom. The new narrative, however, will not be handed down from on high. It will not be constructed by any 'Task Force on Re-Imagining the Episcopal Church' or developed by any strategic planning initiative. The future contours of the Church will emerge as we follow Jesus in new ways and, empowered by the Holy Spirit, try on many different experiments in God's mission of restoration and reconciliation. Our developing, post-Christendom narrative will be discovered as we live the ancient, pre-Christendom vocations as disciples and apostles in the world in new ways.

The vocation to live as disciples of Jesus and serve him as apostles of the Godly reign he came to establish is given to us in Baptism. In Baptism we are both joined to our creator God in the life, death and Resurrection of Jesus and sent out into the world in the power of the Holy Spirit to participate in God's mission. Dying to our old self in the waters of Baptism and rising to new life in Jesus, we own anew our calling as followers of Jesus – disciples of Jesus in a new age. Sealed with the Holy Spirit and marked as Christ's own forever, we are sent into the world as missionaries – apostles of the mission of God. Baptism is all about becoming disciples and apostles in the here and now.

The Baptismal Covenant[31] is an invitation to own our vocation as disciples and apostles. In the first three questions of the Covenant, we are asked: do we believe in God, Father, Son, and Holy Spirit? When we answer using the words of the Apostles' Creed, we affirm our calling to be disciples of, followers of, God in Jesus through the power of the Holy Spirit. The five post-creedal questions that follow are about how we are to be apostles in the world, sent out in God's mission. As we promise, with God's help, to live lives dedicated to worship, forgiveness, evangelism, service, and justice-making, we own our vocation to be about the saving work of the Triune God: we join in God's work of restoring all people to unity with God and each other in Christ. In the promises of the Baptismal Covenant we own our calling to be disciples and apostles of God's mission in a changing world and Church.

31 See: www.episcopalchurch.org/page/baptismal-covenant.

In the Episcopal Church Diocese of Connecticut we are indeed experiencing the realities of the end of Christendom. And, by in large, we are embracing the changes that post-Christendom is bringing forth. Relying on the leading of the Holy Spirit, we are increasingly trying on experiments as followers of Jesus and missionaries in the new world. Our new narrative of the post-Christendom Church has not yet been fully articulated. There is much work ahead of us.

What is needed as we move forward into God's changing world as a changing Church is greater formation as disciples and apostles in God's mission. The future is pregnant with possibilities. Lay and ordained leaders in the Episcopal Church in Connecticut are already actively engaged in imagining, and trying on, new ways in which we all can be formed and resourced as disciples and apostles.

The post-Christendom future is already here in North America. We all are called to be disciples and apostles in God's mission in this changing world and Church.

Chapter 13 – An Anglican Discipleship among Children and Youth

> If our obedience to Jesus includes making 'disciples of all nations', then how do our current attitudes and actions towards children and youth propel us towards this great task? This question is critical for global mission, especially given that almost half of the population of the world is less than 25 years of age and a third of the population is children under 15 years. (*Anne-Christine Bataillard*)

The traditional method of developing the spirituality of our children is by sending them to Sunday school. This is done whether the parents are practising Christians or not. We have relied on volunteers with limited or no training to lead the children for about an hour per week, expecting that the children will get a great spiritual development, sufficiently preparing them for Confirmation and the life beyond.

One of our learnings during youth development is that youth leaders 'burn out' easily because they are unable to cope with the dysfunctionality of the teenagers, primarily because they lack a firm spiritual foundation themselves. This helped us in the Anglican Church of Southern Africa (ACSA) to realize that it was incredibly important to lay a solid foundation during the early years (from age 3 onwards) and to ensure that we develop a seamless ministry through the ages of 3 to 19.

Consequently, we developed a project to develop a new spiritual development framework (in other words a discipleship process) that would cover the lesson themes that need to be covered, as well as provide a toolbox of resources which teachers could use to supplement their lessons. The framework would also include the Sunday school teacher training curriculum.

This project will not seek to re-invent the wheel, but will plug in existing resources and initiatives where they add the most value. These include Godly Play, Rooted in Jesus, Messy Church, and others. But programmes on their own are not enough. The teacher needs to understand how the child or youth develops and will need to be trained to meet the developmental needs appropriately and contextually.

Our understanding of how a holistic approach could be taken was greatly enhanced by the Compassion International Global Advocacy Forum, which advocates for a holistic child development approach, having been doing so for over sixty years.

> Compassion International is a child-advocacy ministry that pairs compassionate people with those who are suffering from poverty. The ministry releases children from spiritual, economic, social, and physical poverty. The goal is for each child to become a responsible and fulfilled adult.[32]

The forum has recently developed ForChildren.com, a website with over 1,400 resource items as well as training which is being made available to the children and youth ministry across the world.

> 'ForChildren.com, presented by Compassion International, offers ideas, learning opportunities and relationships to help equip people who work with children-at-risk. We are a worldwide community of Jesus-followers who are committed to the holistic development of children.'[33]

Considering that *all* children could be considered to be 'at risk' (e.g. even through bullying at school, etc.), then these resources will be useful in any context, and particularly in Africa.

32 Taken from Compassion.com.

33 Taken from Compassion.com.

Chapter 14 – The Bible, Worship, Sacraments, and the Eucharistic Community

For all Christians the primary sources for developing their life together of discipleship and disciple-making are the Christian Scripture studied together within the worship and sacramental life of the faith community. Together the Old and New Testaments provide a complete and sufficient, God-inspired, guide to Christian living, a template for discipleship. Throughout Christian history the Bible has been received as primarily a community document to be read and interpreted within the context of historic Christian communities. Although Christian disciples are encouraged to read the Scriptures privately, the authoritative context for interpretation is always within the worship life of the community.

Unlike some other religious texts, the Christian Scriptures are infinitely translatable and are to be used by each local Christian community, as far as possible, in their mother tongue and in the context of their local daily Christian discipleship. This local use of Scripture is then moderated and critiqued by the interpretive experience of the universal Church across space and time. The current 'Bible in the Life of the Church' programme of the Anglican Communion is a major resource for discipleship in this respect.[34]

As stated in Part A of this book, discipleship is primarily a corporate activity and its ultimate purpose is the glory of God. It is not surprising therefore that alongside our study and use of Scriptures we find that Christian worship and especially the Sacraments are a major resource for discipleship as well as disciple-making. The Christian Sacraments mark significant points of transition on the way of discipleship. Baptism and Confirmation help us with those sometimes challenging new beginnings in life; the Eucharist and the Sacrament of Penance become our regular points of nourishment along the way; Holy Matrimony and Ordination strengthen us for new discipleship responsibilities; and the Anointing of

34 See Percy, Amos, and Markham (eds.), The Bible in the Life of the Church. Also find various resources at: www.anglicancommunion.org/mission/theology/the-bible-in-the-life-of-the-church/further-resources.aspx.

the Sick and Dying helps us enter into the discipleship of the one who comes closest to the Master in suffering. In our daily worship, in the singing of psalms, in our prayer we allow ourselves to be shaped by the One we follow, his life flowing into ours as we seek to draw others into that same intimacy of divine fellowship.

The concept of Eucharistic Community, as taught within the Orthodox spiritual tradition, is much wider than the community gathered around the Lord's Table on a Sunday. It speaks of a community of disciples (both locally and globally) who are gathered around the Lord in constant thanks and praise (Rev 7.9–17). As such we find ourselves empowered by him and one another to live lives that are counter-cultural, radical, and shaped by Christ rather than the values of the contexts in which we live. More than any course or book our daily experience of Eucharistic Community is a rich and challenging resource for intentional discipleship and disciple-making.

Chapter 15 – Resourcing Discipleship?

This chapter provides insights, through stories of lived experience, of how Anglicans are grappling with the reality of being equipped as disciples of Jesus Christ in the twenty-first century in various contexts within the global Communion.

As already mentioned in Part A of this book, discipleship and disciple-making are not about study, courses, or programmes for personal spiritual development or church growth but about our relationship with Jesus Christ and the implications of that relationship in our lived experience, and the stories shared here reflect some of the experiences of Anglicans in their journey of response to the call of their Master.

The Alpha course

The Alpha course is used primarily by churches as a tool for evangelization. To date 27 million people have been through an Alpha course. Alpha has been run in 169 countries, is translated into 112 languages, and is used by most denominations and traditions within the Church globally. Its stated aim is to equip the Church to help people encounter God through Jesus Christ.

In 2014 54 per cent of the people who did Alpha were in Asia, where Alpha has its regional training hub in Kuala Lumpur. Along with the Alpha course there are also Alpha resources to help churches to reach youth.[35]

However, Alpha began in 1978 as an evangelistic and discipleship tool, aimed at new believers and developed by an Anglican Church in London, Holy Trinity Brompton. Discipleship is a lifelong journey, and no one course can accomplish it. This is why Alpha is called Alpha and not the 'Alpha to Omega' course! Some churches, as well as using this tool for evangelization, also use Alpha for discipleship purposes.

35 See www.alpha.org.

There are certain elements of the format and content of Alpha which make it helpful in the discipleship process. Firstly, guests are placed into small groups of up to twelve people (typically two hosts, two helpers, and eight guests). The guests stay in the same small group throughout the duration of the ten-week course. Discipleship is something best done in community, and is not meant to be a solitary journey. Alpha embraces this.

Secondly, the Alpha small group discussion is based on questions. After the presentation from the front on the topic for the week, the small group host asks questions, to which the guests are free to say what they think and feel; they are also free to ask their own questions of one another. Jesus used questions to disciple his followers.

Thirdly, the small group dynamic fosters a sense of belonging. Discipleship happens most fruitfully within the security of feeling that you belong. Many guests on Alpha courses speak of feeling that they belonged before they believed.

Fourthly, discipleship takes time. It is a journey. While Alpha may just be the beginning of a lifelong journey for many, it runs for ten to eleven weeks and allows time and space for people to come to faith and to begin their journey as a disciple.

Fifthly, Alpha begins to model to the guests some of the praxis and spiritual disciplines involved in discipleship, such as reading the Bible, praying, singing, and discussing. The content of the teaching also centres around the Trinity, with topics such as 'Who is Jesus?', 'Why did Jesus die?', 'How can I have faith?', and 'Who is the Holy Spirit?'

Finally, discipleship also involves doing. We grow as we serve; it is not just about consuming. Alpha helps the Church mobilize many in the congregation to help in the process of evangelization, not just the 'natural' evangelists. People can serve by cooking the food, hosting or helping in the small groups, helping to register the guests, putting out the chairs, and of course inviting their friends to come. In this way Alpha helps grow people and also identify talented, emerging leaders.

In time the guests also are initiated into Christian service with the church and wider community.

Rooted in Jesus Junior

Rooted in Jesus Junior (RinJ Junior), designed for use with children aged 8–14, is a parallel programme to Rooted in Jesus (RinJ) for adults;[36] it provides the first systematic Christian syllabus for use in Sunday schools. As with the adult programme, the emphasis is on helping children to trust and follow Jesus in practical ways in their daily lives.

RinJ has now been adopted by sixty-six Anglican dioceses in fifteen African countries stretching from South Sudan to South Africa, as well as by various other denominational networks. It is used for small discipleship groups within local churches, for evangelism and church planting, and for Confirmation preparation and lay ministry training. It can also be used as a follow-on from an evangelistic programme such as Alpha. RinJ Junior was first piloted in 2010, and is now in use in Uganda, South Africa, Zambia, and Tanzania. Both programmes are introduced to a church by an experienced team through a residential training conference, and are supported in each diocese by a diocesan coordinator appointed by the Bishop.[37]

The God Who is There

The God Who is There (TGWIT) grew out of the need for similarly practical and relational discipleship training for use in more developed contexts. It is a three-part small group programme based on the principles of RinJ but giving greater attention to the issues and challenges raised by Western culture. The first part, 'Beyond Ourselves', invites participants to discover a living relationship with God; the second, 'The New Community',

36 See Chapter 9 above.
37 Rooted in Jesus is edited and directed by Alison Morgan and published in the UK by ReSource. In South Africa it is implemented and supported through Growing the Church, and in Tanzania it is directed from his office in Arusha by Bishop Stanley Hotay. Its website is www.rootedinjesus.net.

helps them to deepen their relationship with God in and through their relationships with one another; the third, 'Shining Like Stars', equips them to live with compassion and integrity as Christians in the community and in the workplace. Scripturally based, TGWIT works through discussion, illustration, practical exercises, worship, and prayer. The three parts may be used successively or independently, and each course includes a group members' booklet which summarizes the material covered and provides practical exercises for use between meetings. As with RinJ, the primary challenges of TGWIT are not academic but spiritual.[38]

Ambassadors for Christ[39]

Too many Christians have not been discipled to be missional people in the contexts of their everyday lives. Mission has normally been presented as an opportunity for the worshipping members of churches to offer their leisure time to support the church-sponsored activities of the paid clergy. There are two reasons for this situation: a theological one and a structural one. Theologically, too many have lived with a sacred–secular divided understanding of what it means to be a follower of Jesus. In many cases the culture of local churches has perpetuated this false understanding that Christians are to be separated from the secular and concern themselves with things sacred. Secondly, too few churches are structured in a way that will enable a community of intentional disciples to be formed.

We are convinced, however, that these issues will not be addressed by adding another programme into the over-crowded calendars of local churches. What is needed is a culture change. For that change to happen, church leaders and congregational members have to take seriously Christ's call to live out the profound implications of following him in every area of life. This will entail the 98 per cent of Christians who are not in paid church work, not only using some of their leisure time for the mission activities of the Church when gathered, but embracing the significance of

38 TGWIT is edited by Roger Morgan and published by ReSource (www.resource-arm.net); so far it is in use primarily in the UK, but also in Switzerland, South Africa (through Growing the Church), New Zealand, and Australia.
39 Facilitated by the London Institute for Contemporary Christianity (LICC).

God's desire to use them in his mission in their scattered contexts, i.e. in the day-to-day lives of individual Christians at home, at work, and at rest.

Out of this radical, but simple, re-focusing of our understanding of mission, there is an emerging focus on two core streams of activity – the front line of the contemporary workplace where large numbers of Christians spend so much of their active life, and the gathered community of the local church which disciples people for the whole of life. This relationship between the gathered and scattered people of God is key to releasing Christians for fruitful discipleship in today's world.[40]

To achieve this, both Christians and church leaders need to be equipped with biblical frameworks, practical resources, and training so that they flourish as followers of Jesus and grow whole-life disciple-making communities.

Individual Christians are to be encouraged to grasp the breadth of all that fruitful missional living entails. This includes, but is not limited to, being a messenger of the Gospel. Christians live to glorify God as his goodness and power are expressed through everyday, fruitful lives in situations that require godly character to be modelled, good work to be made, and grace and love to be ministered, and that need a mouthpiece for truth and justice.

As the missional imagination of the Church extends, a new challenge comes into focus. Leading a church into whole-life discipleship requires leaders to become competent in creating interdependency between two main expressions of the church body – as gathered and scattered. Leaders resonate deeply with the need for whole-life mission but find that the main roadblock to becoming such a community is the existing culture of the Church. In this case the Church leaders need to be supported in their efforts to create a disciple-making culture by identifying and implementing a series of manageable changes whose cumulative effect enables a church to become a whole-life disciple-making community.

40 The LICC has developed resources to help churches and church leaders equip Christians to be whole disciples.

The experience is that churches, regardless of their specific confessional traditions, can become communities that envision, equip, and sustain missional disciples of Christ – wherever they may find themselves.

Chapter 16 – Mission and Development Agencies

Whole-life discipleship and the Faith2Share network

Faith2Share is a global network of mission agencies from many different denominations but including a high percentage of the Anglican Communion mission agencies. Established in 2000, the network has a threefold focus on discipleship, collaboration, and emerging mission movements.

In 2011 the leaders of Faith2Share member agencies identified a significant gap in their joint ministries. With considerable resources committed to evangelism, church planting, leadership training, community development, education, and health ministries, they were all experiencing considerable church growth, especially in the Majority World, but failing to see maturity in discipleship. The Rwandan genocide a decade previously had been a wake-up call in Africa, but corruption and nepotism in Asia and the consumerization, nominalism, and moral malaise of the Church in Europe and North America all pointed to a need to address discipleship within the Churches. As a response, in 2012, Faith2Share launched a series of consultations on whole-life discipleship or 'Depth Discipleship'.

Depth Discipleship consultations have now been held in several different locations around the world and more are planned. Each one gathers mission and church leaders to work together on the development of strategies for whole-life discipleship in their region of the world. In outline the consultations address three aspects of life to discover what it means to be a disciple of Jesus in each. The first concerns family (marriage and children), clan, and tribal issues. The second revolves around relations of employment, our use of money, etc., and the third looks at community issues, politics, the environment, and inter-faith relationships. In each context participants decide which issues are significant for effective discipleship in their own context.

In facilitating this process Faith2Share has deliberately not produced any handbooks or teaching materials but only a framework for consultation. The issues, resources, and session facilitators are all chosen locally to ensure that the process is fully contextualized and locally appropriate. The aim is to develop processes within churches and mission agencies that lead to a maturity of discipleship in which Anglican and other Christians are enabled to follow the ways of Jesus in every aspect of their lives.

Insider movements and discipleship

One major development in the world of mission over the past two decades has been the emergence of, and increasing debate about, so-called insider movements. But to what exactly does the term 'insider movement' refer?

While several definitions have been put forth in the literature, we here adopt the definition used by Anglicans most intimately involved with these movements, i.e. authentically biblical movements to Jesus which were able to remain 'within' various religious traditions and combine the dynamics of people movements or mass movements,[41] with elements of what has been referred to by some as C-5.[42]

As such, the core elements of an insider movement include:

(a) Saving faith in Jesus Christ;

41 See, for example, Donald McGavran, The Bridges of God (New York: Friendship Press, 1955); J. Waskom Pickett, Christian Mass Movements in India: A Study (New York: Abingdon Press, 1933); and Alan R. Tippett, People Movements in Southern Polynesia (Chicago: Moody Press, 1971).

42 The C-Scale is described in John Travis, 'Must All Muslims Leave Islam to Follow Jesus?', Evangelical Missions Quarterly, 34/4 (1998), pp. 407–8. Most practitioners, including Travis himself, are moving away from the C-Scale, or at least distinguish between C-5 and 'insider movements'. We refer to C-5 here as a convenience. In fact, the kind of movements we are describing would have to be described as a mix of C-4 and C-5 if we were to use the C-Scale to evaluate them. See also the discussions in Timothy C. Tennent, Theology in the Context of World Christianity (Grand Rapids, MI: Zondervan, 2007) and Kevin Higgins, 'Identity, Integrity and Insider Movements: A Brief Paper Inspired by Timothy C. Tennent's Critique of C5 Thinking', International Journal of Frontier Missions, 23/3 (2006), pp. 117–23.

(b) Commitment to living under biblical authority;

(c) (The development of contextually appropriate forms of ekklesia;

(d) A decision to remain within at least some aspects of the religion of one's birth.

How does discipleship take place in this sort of movement? There are two key elements to the discipleship that takes place within the two largest movements we know of:

(a) Disciples are formed by being part of small believing communities, or 'house churches', which meet mainly for believers. These small *ekklesia* units pray together, read and discuss the Scriptures, and share simple expressions of the Lord's Supper.

(b) Disciples are also formed as they take part in 'leadership' training clusters. The primary focus of such groups is the reading and hearing and application of the portions of the Bible as we have them, mutual prayer, encouragement, and ongoing planning for, and participation in, the expansion of the movement through evangelism and the planting of more groups.

The descriptions here should serve to dispel the common misperception that insider movements are underground, hiding, afraid, or even subversive and deceptive.[43] In fact the movements known to us are focused on evangelism and the planting of house churches.

Another feature of the discipleship that takes place in insider movements is the process of how believers engage with the religion of their birth. All

43 For more about insider movements from multiple perspectives see Kevin Higgins, 'The Key to Insider Movements', International Journal of Frontier Missions, 21/4 (2004), pp. 155–65. See also discussions published in St Francis Magazine, especially Higgins, '"Inside What?" Church, Culture, Religion and Insider Movements in Biblical Perspective', St Francis Magazine, 5/4 (August 2009), pp. 74–91, with Responses by Bill Nikides and 'Phil' on pp. 91–113 and 114–26, and then the response by Higgins in St Francis Magazine, 5/6 (December 2009), pp. 61–86.

disciples, of course, wrestle with how their pre-disciple life and their life as a disciple interface. But this is of particular sensitivity when one seeks to live within as much of one's birth religion as is biblically faithful. Since there is not room to address this in detail, a summary must suffice. There are several dimensions. As disciples begin to seek obedience to Jesus in the Scriptures they tend to make one of several choices related to past religious actions, ceremonies, etc.:

(a) Reject: There are some things which become very clear to the disciple that must be rejected, for example, the use of magic or curses or charms to effect spiritual impact.

(b) Retain: Certain actions or practices are neutral, or what the reformers may have called adiaphora. In Christian settings, Christmas trees have taken this sort of place for many in spite of their pagan roots. For some insider disciples, this may involve clothing, beards, etc.

(c) Re-interpret: In some cases a practice or rite might be continued but given new meaning. An example has been the slaughter of an animal during Muslim Eid celebrations, which in some cases is now re-interpreted to remind believers of the Ultimate Sacrifice made for us on the Cross.

(d) Re-value: In other instances a practice might be kept but relegated to lesser or perhaps greater importance. An example of the former has been the sometimes legalistic way in which Muslims might keep the five-times-daily prayers. In some cases disciples keep to that practice, but without giving it the importance it used to have (this is also a case where re-interpretation happens, as the content of the prayers often changes as well). But in some cases practices such as giving to the poor become even more important than previously.

As for every disciple of Jesus, discipleship within insider movements is a process. It is a process that happens over time, within community, and through intentional and prayerful engagement with Scripture and lived experience.

Fresh expressions of Church and discipleship

Methodology and notation

Since 2011, Church Army's research unit has been collecting quantitative data on all known fresh expressions of Church, including church plants. Longitudinal data is provided in that the research covers all those started in the period 1992–2014. As of July 2015 the team has full records for sixteen of the forty-one English dioceses, and it aims to complete records for twenty-one dioceses in this cycle. In this section the phenomenon known as fresh expressions of Church is abbreviated to fxC.

This research included a specific question about four common approaches taken to foster discipleship. Because it is quantitative work there is a distinct limit to the depth of enquiry. In addition, the section that follows does not cover other related researched steps in discipleship that these young churches or fxC have taken. These include use of the Bible in worship, observance of the two dominical Sacraments, how they are engaging in evangelism, or steps they have taken towards their individual responsibility.[44]

In research carried out by telephone, the leader(s) of each fxC were asked to indicate whether discipleship among those drawn to fxC used any or all of the following: small groups, one-to-one meetings, running courses, and serving in teams. Thus far the research team have replies from 833 fxC, all of which met criteria set for being truly fxC – that is, they were both missional and ecclesial.[45]

44 More details about all examples from the first eleven dioceses can be found at: www.churcharmy.org.uk\fxCresearch.

45 The ten criteria used are available from Church Army, email: ask@churcharmy.org.uk.

The findings or 'letters from young churches'

Readers should realize that here we are dealing with small, young, varied churches. Most are under five years old, their average size is forty-four, and there are probably about twenty different types of fxC. They were started in all kinds of social contexts, from city centre to deeply rural, and they arise from the width of the traditions of the Church of England. Thus there are many aspects that nuance the findings.

The clear headline is that across the sixteen dioceses, 78 per cent of the fxC are taking some steps in discipleship, while 22 per cent describe themselves as not at this stage. It is not the case that discipleship is peripheral to fxC. Always the majority are doing something about it. It would take qualitative work to assess its effect and whether it might be thought sufficient.

There are significant findings, depending on which other factor is considered besides steps in discipleship. The clearest is the connection to frequency of meeting. Across all four paths tracked, those that meet weekly are most likely to have chosen at least one of them, then those that meet fortnightly, and last those meeting monthly. The mitigating factor is that progress towards marks of maturity is likely to take longer in monthly gatherings. Depth of relationship, establishing patterns of belonging, and securing commitment do take time. 89 per cent of the weekly fxC had engaged in discipleship, and 84 per cent of the fortnightly ones, but only 66 per cent of the monthly ones.

There is also a clear correlation with the type of area served, but this factor will affect resources available and the resultant frequency of meeting and perhaps choice of type of fxC. The nine kinds of urban area listed consistently scored better for steps in discipleship than the two rural ones: expanded villages and (deeper) rural areas. The differences at the ends of spectrum are shown by fxC in city centres being nearly twice as likely to have taken particular steps as fxC in rural areas and expanded villages. The best scoring in all four approaches were fxC in city centres. The provision of small groups turned out to be more common in towns and private housing estates than in deprived urban areas. Serving in teams was prominent in suburbs and towns, while meeting one-to-one was more common in deprived urban contexts than in the towns, private estates, and suburbs. We suggest this means that choices are being made according to context; this is affected by venues available, social expectations, ability to travel, and preferred learning styles.

Types of church tradition also make a difference to the four discipleship choices selected. We asked people if those who started the fxC identified with any, or up to three, traditions out of five cited. Consistently those in the charismatic tradition scored best in all four measures, and then came the Evangelicals. Those in the Central, Anglo-Catholic, or Liberal tradition came next, depending on the discipleship measure chosen. We also scored for combinations of the traditions, and here the charismatic and evangelical traditions scored the best of all. We doubt that the predetermined choices unduly affected these results, but suggest they link with preferences for encouraging the ministry of the laity.

At that point it is also clear that there are minimal differences in steps taken in discipleship between different groups who lead: those fxC led by ordained ministers, those led by all laity, and those led by unauthorized and untrained laity. Each group is exactly as likely to have encouraged attenders to have taken some steps in discipleship. Clergy are more likely to favour running groups and offering courses, with the laity favouring one-to-one meeting. This may reflect time available.

Last we come to connections between approaches to discipleship and types of fxC. Some strong links are inherent. So all cell churches have small groups and score well on serving in teams but have little need for one-to-one meetings. Clusters, sometimes called mission-shaped communities, similarly score well on one-to-one meetings, small groups, and serving in teams because these are their values. It was more of a surprise that churches begun for networks score well on all four measures, for their membership is more geographically dispersed. Other kinds of fxC such as church among under-fives were likely to score badly on small groups and serving in teams, but better on courses (such as parenting) and one-to-one meetings. Other low-scoring kinds were church for older people – except for one-to-one meetings – and midweek congregations. It is of concern that the three most common kinds, Messy Church, Café Church, and child-focused church do not score highly on discipleship. The Messy Church scores are 21 per cent for small groups and the same for courses, 30 per cent for serving in teams, and 39 per cent for one-to-one meetings. But the vast majority of them are monthly gatherings, which may be equally diagnostic.

A wider picture

These data are reasonably robust but can only be an introduction. There are other bigger questions. The data show that the fxC engage with more de-churched and non-churched people than other groups, and we do not know exactly how this should affect the processes and content of disciple-making and maturing. It is likely to take longer and start further back. This journey still lacks some waymarks.

The wider Church is also recalibrating discipleship through the lens of different ways to learn. Some cite three kinds: formal or academic, non-formal or apprenticeship, and socialization typical of the family. It is arguable that too much in the past has been through the first. It is good that the term 'apprenticeship' occurs in Chapter 9 of this book, and it will mesh with the healthy rise of the laity.

It is also arguable that the telos of discipleship needs connecting to the exalted early Church call to theosis. We do not just follow Jesus, but are called to be transformed in character, priorities, and virtue to become like him. All this will take more research to discover what progress is being made.

Chapter 17 – Conclusion: The Case for Intentional Discipleship in the Communion

This book has demonstrated theologically and practically the need to intentionally recognize God-given gifts in all the baptized and to equip them in order to bring people to follow Jesus Christ as Lord and Saviour and become lifelong disciples within the community of God's people and in the wider world.

Why discipleship and disciple-making need to be intentional

While evangelism was always present among Anglicans, there is some validity in stating that the period of emphasis on evangelism, famously known as the Decade of Evangelism, was instrumental in creating or awakening the consciousness of many Anglicans to make evangelism an intentional business.

Although the Decade of Evangelism was not the only factor in promoting evangelism, and certainly not every Anglican diocese or province embraced the imagination of the Communion-wide call for emphasis on evangelism, many Anglicans, however, look back to that period as the catalyst for growth in church attendance and church planting.

In the survey made in preparation for the 2008 Lambeth Conference, it was evident that in other parts of the Communion, the decline in church membership and church attendance was the catalyst for intentional focus on evangelism and church growth work.

The numerical growth of churches, particularly in the Global South – Africa, Asia, and Latin America – has been a cause for celebration, but as some leaders have already acknowledged, an increase of numbers in church attendance has not made significant change in people's commitment to church life and community transformation.[46]

46 See examples below.

In light of the above, it goes without saying that a dedicated period, such as a Season of Intentional Discipleship and Disciple-Making, has the potential to catalyse renewal and transformation in the Anglican Communion. It must be stated that the vision to focus on intentional discipleship and disciple-making is not intended to address poor church attendance, nor is it aimed at countering the challenge faced by churches with high attendance and yet low commitment and community compact, although both would be by-products of it, but that the biblical call to 'make disciples' is to honour and glorify God, as Christians live out their faith in everyday life as faithful followers of Jesus Christ, their Lord and Master.[47]

The time or time frame is not the object or intended goal of this vision but simply a means to instil within the consciousness of Anglicans the intentionality to own what must come natural and is central to Christianity and Christian living and witness.

Why discipleship and disciple-making are not only biblical but also Anglican

This book has adequately articulated the biblical and theological case for discipleship and disciple-making. An exploration of what the Instruments of Communion have said about discipleship and disciple-making in Part A of this book also clearly shows that discipleship is the DNA of the Anglican Communion. The Communion is the child of mission, born as Anglican Christians travelled to new places to invite others to become disciples of Jesus Christ.

Discipleship is the very essence of Anglicanism. Anglicanism, from its roots in Celtic and Augustinian spirituality and shaped by the European Reformation, has always been a lived-out (not a purely intellectual or spiritualized) faith. It is about following and living the ways of Jesus.

47 Mt 28.18–20; Jn 15.8.

Discipleship is the way Anglicans witness to Jesus. Anglican witness is holistic: it is about proclamation, service, worship, and prophetic witness as a way of living as citizens of the Kingdom in this world, disciples of the Crucified One.

Discipleship reflects the Catholic-Protestant nature of the Anglican Communion. We discover the true meaning of the Catholic nature of the Church as we follow a Saviour who unites all people, all things, in himself, and we discover the true vocation of Protestantism as our discipleship leads us into a prophetic engagement with all that is not holy.

Discipleship is the future of the Anglican Communion. It is only as we call each generation anew to a daily walk with God, a living discipleship, that the Anglican Church can grow or even survive. Without new disciples our future is no longer than one generation.

Discipleship is the hope of the Anglican Communion. It is only through calling all Anglicans, and those who will join as new Christians, to a daily following of Christ that we will avoid error, division, and distraction and know the constant renewal of the Spirit that gives hope for eternity.

At a period in its history when the Anglican Communion is experiencing division, decline, and growth (in different regions, but also side by side) and theological challenge, it will not retain its relevance in contemporary society and the Kingdom through discipline, debate, or even discourse alone, but primarily through the deepening of the discipleship of all members in every aspect of their lives, in every place. Discipleship is the lifeblood of the Anglican Communion.

Why we need a Communion-wide focus on discipleship and disciple-making

The Christian Body (the Church) is experiencing the most interesting of times in history with unique opportunities for Christian witness largely brought about by the challenges that divide and the technology that connects the peoples of our time.

In this twenty-first century there has been a growing realization of the huge potential that the Christian faith has to transform local and global communities set against the reality of the lack of, or diminished impact of, Christian faith on human character even in areas where Christians are present in huge numbers.

While making disciples is Christ's mandate given to his followers and those after them, in recent decades, in the Anglican community and in some other traditions, there has been very little intentional emphasis on equipping, mentoring, forming, teaching, or maturing and recognizing the gifts of those who believe in Jesus (all the baptized) to be lifelong disciples whose faith is to have impact in or influence every sphere of their daily experience.[48]

Even where Christianity is still popular in terms of numbers, the effectiveness of its members is often minimal, and can also be described as nominal and minority. In other areas there is a growing danger that faith becomes a private matter, a personal moral exercise, rather than a whole-life-shaping discipleship in devotion and obedience to Christ, lived in the context of everyday life.

The following quotations from Anglican leaders and those of other churches are indicative of the prevailing challenge and the gap that exists between professed faith and lived faith:

> We have no problem filling our churches with people, but they need to know what it means to be Christians (followers of Jesus), that is where we need help. (Archbishop David Vunagi, former Primate of the Anglican Church of Melanesia)

48 The command to 'make disciples of all nations' (Mt 28.19) must go hand in hand with emphasis on how disciples ought to live their life. 'You shall love the Lord your God with all your heart, and with all your soul, and with all your mind … And a second is like it: "You shall love your neighbour as you love yourself"' (Mt 22.37–39; Mk 12.28–34; Lk 10.25–28). 'You are the light of the world. A city built on a hill cannot be hidden' (Mt 5.14). 'You are the salt of the earth' (Mt 5.13).

Kajo-Keji is known as a Christian community. Greet someone in the street and you will find they have a Christian name. But how deep and strong a faith in Jesus Christ does that person have? It is very likely they do not have the impact on the community that, as salt and light, Jesus wants us to have. This is partly because we often focus on reaping a harvest of souls without going on to make disciples, as Jesus commanded us to in the Great Commission (Mt 28.19). The Diocese of Kajo-Keji is attempting to put that right. (Kajo-Keji Diocese, South Sudan)

One of the themes which emerged from the conversations distilled in Capital Vision 2020 was a repeated call for ways of equipping people more effectively to live and speak the Gospel of Jesus Christ in their everyday lives. (London Diocese Bishops, Lent 2014)

We have many Christians but part-time disciples, many pastors but part-time disciples. (Archbishop Ng Moon Hing, Bishop of West Malaysia and Primate of South East Asia)

The Church often attracts the best people but soon turns them into bureaucrats by putting them on the committees, and not long, they start complaining because they have nothing to do … The Church is a sleeping giant. (Pastor Sam Ko, SaRang Community Church, South Korea)

The absence of any real emphasis upon discipleship in England in the 1930s, 40s, and 50s had a profound impact on the decline we are experiencing today. (Archbishop Justin Welby)

A lot of people are confirmed by the Bishop but their commitment to the Church remains very low. (Bishop David Njovu, Lusaka Diocese, Zambia)

> In 2012 the Church in Wales embarked on a 2020 Vision, which emerged out of introspection in the light of the expected commemoration in 2020 of 100 years since the Church was disestablished. The review report acknowledged 'a moment of crisis' in the Church, and identified the 'shortage of ordinands' and the structures that are not able to connect with young people and the wider society in general as some of the alarm bells that has prompted the Church to embark on a 'creative response to what Christ is asking of us at this time'.[49]

Anglicans and Episcopalians all over the world are witnessing to Christ's reconciling love in all sorts of ways and circumstances, a sign of commitment to discipleship. However, many leaders in the Anglican Communion will also identify themselves with the above remarks, and many others recognize that we could have done better if we had put more resources in and focused on nurturing and equipping, not only new believers but existing ones too, to deepen their discipleship and Christian witness. Many leaders are seeing discipleship as central to real growth and the potential to transforming society with the Gospel of Christ.

Therefore the real question is not whether or not something is being done but rather what value a coordinated Communion-wide movement, that is intentional, could add to what is happening rather than doing things in isolation.

Thus the need for a Communion-wide period of emphasis on intentional discipleship, intentional equipping of all the baptized members to live out their faith with their gifts and skills in everyday life as Christ's ambassadors, is both necessary and urgent.

There is need to mobilize and disseminate experience, good practice, and resources, and to promote collaboration and learning from each other, so

49 See the review report at: www.churchinwales.org.uk/review/report/.

as to build up the Body of Christ in its witness to Christ's reconciling love today (and tomorrow).

It is important to appreciate that putting emphasis on intentional discipleship will have implications for the whole life of the Church, including its structures, liturgy, prayer and worship, selection and training of ordination candidates, and leadership formation and deployment in general, etc., and it will have to be aligned in accord with this vision.